OTHER FORUM FOR THE FUTURE OF HIGHER EDUCATION PUBLICATIONS

FORUM FUTURES: 2000 PAPERS

FORUM FUTURES

Exploring the Future of Higher Education, 2000 Papers

Forum Strategy Series, Volume 3

Maureen Devlin, Joel Meyerson, Editors

JOSSEY-BASS
A Wiley Company
San Francisco

Jossey-Bass books and products are available through most bookstores. To contact Jossey-Bass directly, call (888) 378-2537, fax to (800) 605-2665, or visit our website at www.josseybass.com.

Substantial discounts on bulk quantities of Jossey-Bass books are available to corporations, professional associations, and other organizations. For details and discount information, contact the special sales department at Jossey-Bass.

 Printed in the United States of America on acid-free, recycled stock that meets or exceeds the minimum GPO and EPA requirements for recycled paper.

Library of Congress Cataloging-in-Publication Data
Futures forum : Exploring the future of higher education, 2000 papers / Maureen Devlin, Joel W. Meyerson, editors. — 1st ed.
    p.   cm. — (The Jossey-Bass higher and adult education series)
Papers from a symposium of the Forum for the Future of Higher Education.
Includes bibliographical references (p.   ) and index.
  ISBN 0-7879-5732-1
  1. Education, Higher—Aims and objectives—United States—Congresses.   2. Universities and colleges—United States—Administration—Congresses.   I. Devlin, Maureen, 1959–
II. Meyerson, Joel W., 1951–   III. Forum for the Future of Higher Education.   IV. Series.
LA227.40.F88   2001
    378.73—dc21   00-012187

FIRST EDITION
PB Printing   10 9 8 7 6 5 4 3 2 1

THE JOSSEY-BASS

HIGHER AND ADULT EDUCATION SERIES

CONTENTS

TABLES, FIGURES, & EXHIBITS

Tables

Figures

Exhibit

FORUM PARTICIPANTS

FORUM FUTURES 2000 PARTICIPANTS

Lloyd Armstrong, University of Southern California

Paul J. Aslanian, Swarthmore College

John H. Augustine, Lehman Brothers

Raymond Bacchetti, The William and Flora Hewlett Foundation

Steve Barclay, University of California, San Francisco

Carol Barone, EDUCAUSE

Nancy Y. Bekavac, Scripps College

Bahram Bekhradnia, Higher Education Funding Council of England

Jerry Berenson, Bryn Mawr College

Clark Bernard, PricewaterhouseCoopers

Wendell C. Brase, University of California, Irvine

Lauren Brisky, Vanderbilt University

Glenn R. Bucher, The Boyer Center

Paula P. Burger, Johns Hopkins University

Carol Campbell, Carleton College

Danielle Carr, The Andrew W. Mellon Foundation

Kent John Chabotar, Bowdoin College

Joseph A. Chalmers, Oracle Corporation

Kristine Chase, Saint Mary's College

Joel G. Clemmer, Macalester College

David Collis, Yale University

Ruth Constantine, Smith College

Robert A. Culnane, Goldman Sachs

Dean W. Currie, Rice University

John R. Curry, Massachusetts Institute of Technology

Jean Cusick, Forum for the Future of Higher Education

John J. DeGioia, Georgetown University

Maureen Devlin, Forum for the Future of Higher Education

James A. Dewar, Rand Corporation

James L. Doti, Chapman University

Ronald G. Ehrenberg, Cornell University

James Engell, Harvard University

Andrew Evans, Oberlin College

Brian Fender, Higher Education Funding Council of England

Keith Finan, Williams College

Gerald B. Finch, The Stillwater Higher Education Group

Joseph Fink, Dominican College of San Rafael

Michael Finlayson, University of Toronto

Robert H. Frank, Cornell University

Craig J. Franz, Saint Mary's College

John A. Fry, University of Pennsylvania

Pamela Gann, Claremont McKenna College

Virginia Gregg, Rensselaer Polytechnic Institute

John S. Griswold, Jr., The Common Fund

Janet C. Hamilton, University of California, Davis

Katharine H. Hanson, Consortium for Financing Higher Education

Brian L. Hawkins, EDUCAUSE

Patrick J. Hennigan, Morgan Stanley Dean Witter

Diana L. Hoadley, J.P. Morgan

Caroline M. Hoxby, Harvard University

Lyn Hutton, The John D. & Catherine T. MacArthur Foundation

William J. Hynes, Saint Mary's College

Weldon E. Ihrig, University of Washington

Richard N. Katz, EDUCAUSE

Patrick Keating, UNEXT.com

Stephen Kelly, Carleton College

V. Wayne Kennedy, University of California System

Karen Kennelly, Mount St. Mary's College

Jillinda J. Kidwell, PricewaterhouseCoopers

Robert W. Kuckuck, Lawrence Livermore National Laboratory

Lucie Lapovsky, Mercy College

Richard C. Larson, Massachusetts Institute of Technology

Steven D. Lavine, California Institute of the Arts

Paul Lawler, W.K. Kellogg Foundation

David A. Lieberman, University of Miami

David Longanecker, Western Interstate Commission for Higher Education

Luther S. Luedtke, California Lutheran University

Edward MacKay, University of New Hampshire

Warren R. Madden, Iowa State University of Science and Technology

William Massy, Stanford University

Nancy Maull, Harvard University

Mary Jo Maydew, Mount Holyoke College

Marilyn McCoy, Northwestern University

James T. McGill, Johns Hopkins University

Mary Patterson McPherson, The Andrew W. Mellon Foundation

Michael McPherson, Macalester College

Michael A. McRobbie, Indiana University

Daniel M. Meyers, First Marblehead Corporation

Joel Meyerson, Forum for the Future of Higher Education

Ted Mitchell, Occidental College

Stephen C. Morgan, University of La Verne

James E. Morley, Jr., NACUBO

Joseph P. Mullinix, Yale University

Michele Tolela Myers, Sarah Lawrence College

Jeanne Narum, Project Kaleidoscope (NSF)

Rosemarie Nassif, Holy Names College

Helen Ouellette, Williams College

Judith G. Palmer, Indiana University

Ronald J. Paprocki, University of Rochester

Margaret F. Plympton, Bucknell University

Fredric J. Prager, Prager, McCarthy & Sealy

Steven Relyea, University of California, San Diego

Henry Riggs, Keck Graduate Institute of Applied Life Sciences

James S. Roberts, Duke University

Frederick A. Rogers, Cornell University

Sean C. Rush, IBM

Morton Schapiro, University of Southern California

Robert Shireman, The James Irvine Foundation

James L. Shulman, The Andrew W. Mellon Foundation

Burton Sonenstein, United Insurance Management Company

Richard Spies, Princeton University

Jon C. Strauss, Harvey Mudd College

Glenn P. Strehle, Massachusetts Institute of Technology

Myra H. Strober, Stanford University

Robert Thompson, Georgia Institute of Technology

Steadman Upham, Claremont University Center & Graduate School

Timothy Warner, Stanford University

J. Fred Weintz, Jr., Stanford University

PREFACE

Maureen E. Devlin

Rapid technological change and intense competition not only define the cutting edge of commerce today but also characterize the current environment in which colleges and universities must function. Technological advances have the potential to deconstruct traditional forms of higher education, as they have allowed for-profit entities and others to provide higher and continuing education outside the conventional university setting and to capture a large share of the burgeoning demand beyond the conventional eighteen- to twenty-one-year-old residential population. Technology and the Internet also present exciting possibilities for advancements in pedagogy, which has remained largely unchanged for centuries.

In this dynamic and ever-changing atmosphere, educational leaders must ground themselves by reexamining the essential purposes of higher learning. To that end, the Forum for the Future of Higher Education convened its annual symposium in the fall of 1999. Forum participants considered the functions and goals of higher education, as well as issues related to strategy, finances, and the effects of technology. This book, *Forum Futures,* summarizes the symposium's presentations and discussions in an effort to help today's leaders address the challenges they face and to shape the future of higher education.

Winner-Take-All Markets

In Chapter One, Robert Frank describes higher education as the quintessential *winner-take-all* market, in which small differences in performance (or even small differences in the credentials used to predict performance) translate into extremely large differences in reward. The effect of such a market is dramatic, influencing many aspects of the academy.

Frank first described these markets in his 1995 book, *The Winner-Take-All Society,* coauthored with Philip Cook. The key characteristic of a winner-take-all environment is that success breeds success and failure breeds failure, all in an ever-strengthening spiral. In higher education, elite universities depend heavily on enrolling top students, who feel just as compelled to enroll in elite institutions. This codependence creates the spirals that amplify the rewards for successfully recruiting top students and faculty. Hierarchical rankings in higher education, which are becoming more visible and important than ever, exacerbate the situation.

Participants in winner-take-all markets face strong incentives to invest in performance enhancement, thereby increasing their chances of coming out on the winning side. Universities have found themselves in an extremely costly positional "arms race," bidding for the various resources that facilitate the quest for high rankings. They are spending more and more on recruiting brochures and videos, nicer dormitories, better food, fancier athletics complexes, and so on. Yet when all schools increase such expenditures, their actions largely cancel one another's out. The additional spending inflates costs but in the end has little impact on the ultimate distribution of students.

Under these circumstances, no institution dares to cut its own expenditures unilaterally. It may be possible, though, to control costs through positional "arms control agreements," pacts in which contestants pledge mutual restraint. Such agreements are particularly important in winner-take-all markets, in which behavior that looks attractive to each individual often looks profoundly unattractive from the perspective of the group. Collusive agreements to restrain these behaviors can create gains for everyone. They should not be summarily judged as wrong based on the uncritical belief that unlimited competition always leads to the greatest good for all.

To move forward and effectively limit escalation in the cost of acquiring higher education, the nature of higher education's winner-take-all market must be recognized, and institutions must be permitted to come together to defuse their positional arms race.

Just as institutions are competing to enroll them, top students are vying to gain entry into the nation's elite colleges and universities. As applications increase, institutions can be more selective about whom they admit, and so the sorting among colleges on the basis of aptitude increases. In Chapter Two, Caroline Hoxby investigates what appears to be a primary driver of the unprecedented numbers of applications—namely, the monetary returns to attending a highly selective college. She reports that the return to education has been increasing since the early 1970s and has been increasing more for people of higher measured aptitude, who today tend to be clustered at selective colleges.

Hoxby divided colleges into eight rank groups based on *Barron's Profiles of American Colleges'* rating of their selectivity. Comparisons of earnings show that men who graduate from more selective colleges tend to earn substantially more by age thirty-two than men who graduate from less selective colleges. Projecting earnings over a lifetime shows, for example, that a typical man who entered a rank 1 private college in 1982 can expect to earn $2.9 million over his career, while a man who entered a rank 8 private college at the same time can expect to earn about $1.75 million over his career. It is obvious that career income differences swamp the differences in the total costs of attending more versus less selective colleges.

Hoxby analyzed earnings for students entering college in 1960, 1972, and 1982 and found that the income differences between rank groups have been growing over time for post-1972 entrants, particularly for more selective colleges. Additionally, comparison of entrants with the same measured aptitude (upon leaving high school) indicates that those who graduate from more selective colleges tend to earn more over their careers.

Monetary returns to attending highly selective colleges have become so great that, surprisingly, most offers of "free rides"—full tuition, room and board, and expenses—are not as good as they seem if one has the option of attending a more selective school, even without financial aid. For example, the data indicate that a graduate could earn back the extra costs of paying full expenses at a rank 1 school within ten years as opposed to accepting a free ride to a rank 3 school. Rank 3 includes Barron's "highly competitive" institutions, such as Carleton, Davidson, Georgetown, and the University of Virginia. Clearly, the winner-take-all phenomenon prevails in this realm as well, where slight differences in aptitude can ultimately lead to great differences in career earnings.

When institutions and students focus on status, recognition, and economic gain as ends in themselves, they diminish additional and important goods derived from the pursuit of education, including social, political, and moral benefits, as well as the pursuit of knowledge for its own sake. In Chapter Three, James Engell presents a model for growth and change in higher education that centers on the *entelechy* of higher education.

Entelechy, stemming from Greek, means the striving for perfection in a series of goals taken together as a whole. For higher education, an entelechy demands we envision how to fulfill the potential of the whole by coordinating and giving proper relative weight to a set of varied goals and the goods these goals seek to achieve. Overemphasis in any particular arena skews the balance of the whole and breaks down fulfillment of its greater potential.

Engell maintains that today higher education's economic good is overemphasized. To illustrate, he identifies three criteria that recently have determined whether an academic field will thrive or languish: (1) a promise of money—the field is linked to improved chances of above average lifetime earnings; (2) a knowledge of money—the field itself studies some aspect of money; and (3) a source of money—the field receives significant research contracts, grants, and so on. The rule of these criteria has been remarkably potent, uniform, and verifiable.

The humanities and several social sciences fail to meet all three criteria. And in the last thirty years, by every term of prestige and quality measured, the humanities have fallen further and further behind other fields. Thus the economic prosperity of the last generation coincides with an overall degradation of the humanities. Yet preservation of the humanities is essential to capturing the lessons of the past and applying them to the future, particularly as we absorb and interpret the effects of science, knowledge, and technology on our inner lives, values, and ideals.

Engell urges higher education leaders to move beyond the current mantra of competition, which begets forces such as the three criteria, to focus again on the essential purposes of higher learning, so that they may direct change from within their institutions rather than merely reacting to the forces of change that surround them.

Defining and Managing Costs

The winner-take-all mentality is no greater in any field than in athletics, where the costs of intercollegiate programs have grown tremendously in the pursuit of victory. Costly competition is also among the several factors that put upward pressure on tuition, whose rise has commanded national attention. Defining the actual costs of athletics programs and higher education in general has proven extremely problematic.

In Chapter Four, James Shulman and William Bowen examine the financial costs of low-profile sports at institutions competing across the range of National Collegiate Athletic Association (NCAA) divisions—from the so-called "big-time" Division I-A level, where in 1997–98 institutions spent an average of $38 million for their athletics programs, to the nonscholarship Division III level, where expenses that year ranged from $1.2 to $1.7 million.

Shulman and Bowen found that for low-profile sports, Division I-A schools spend nearly ten times as much per team as the Division III colleges, and the Ivies spend three times as much per team as the Division III schools. Thus even outside the arena of big-time football and men's basketball, the level of play chosen by an institution has a significant financial impact.

Shulman and Bowen also compared the SAT scores of athletes with those of the rest of the student body. They found large gaps across all competitive levels between the student body and high-profile sport athletes (football, men's basketball, and men's ice hockey players); the largest gap (284 points) was in the Division I-A private universities. Smaller gaps were found between the student body and participants in low-profile sports, ranging from 25 points at the Division III level to about 120 points at the Division I-A private schools. Historical data show that these gaps have been growing over time.

Shulman and Bowen point to the competitive pressures of intercollegiate athletics, which relentlessly drive up costs in a race that never ends. The situation is exacerbated by the common misperception that athletics teams or programs are no-cost goods. While direct costs may be recognized, capital and administrative costs, as well as trade-offs in admissions decisions, are often overlooked. The authors urge collective action to slow the seemingly endless raising of the stakes in college sports, which in the end does not seem to achieve any optimal goal. This process must begin with a clear understanding of the financial facts and a strong sense of the missions of the institutions engaged in intercollegiate competition.

The high visibility and enormous appeal of college sports lead many to believe that successful football and men's basketball programs more than pay for themselves. Yet the most recent NCAA data report that in 1997 less than half of the Division I-A programs (43 percent) reported "profits," and the average "deficit" at the remaining programs was $2.8 million.

Another common misperception is that successful intercollegiate programs stimulate alumni giving. Yet Shulman found no evidence that variations in the won-lost records of the Division I-A or the Ivy League institutions he studied had any effect on alumni giving.

Financial data about intercollegiate athletics can be extremely obscure, making its analysis quite difficult. For example, in the same year that Duke's federal reporting form showed that athletics revenues exceeded expenditures by $2 million, institutional transfers to athletics were in the $4 to $5 million range.

Campus leaders must have access to clear and accurate financial information to make informed decisions about their institutions' athletics programs. Armed with such data, they can effectively assess and implement priorities among various interests across campus competing for limited funds. Beyond campus, educational leaders must work together to forge the collective agreements essential to containing the athletics "arms race" and the high costs of intercollegiate competition.

Similar to the pressures and outside scrutiny focused on highly visible intercollegiate athletics programs, tuition levels have become subject to intense, national-level discussion and debate. In Chapter Five, Ronald Ehrenberg assesses upward pressures on tuition, particularly at selective private colleges and universities, in research funded by the Andrew W. Mellon Foundation. His findings point toward several recommendations to help hold down costs.

Among the cost pressures on tuition, Ehrenberg notes first the winner-take-all higher education market, wherein selective institutions compete, at great expense, to be the very best in every aspect of their activities. In the same vein, highly visible rankings give institutions every incentive to improve their rank despite the costs associated with such efforts.

The shared governance system, too, between trustees, administrators, and faculty virtually guarantees that private institutions will be slow to react to pressure to reduce costs. Trustees should be encouraged to look beyond their special interests and play a strong role in backing the efforts of presidents and provosts to reduce costs.

Several federal government policies also contribute to cost pressures, among them the breakup of the collective agreement of several elite schools to target their financial aid to students with the greatest need, rather than offer merit aid, and the pressure on research institutions to lower their indirect costs rates.

Institutions' budgetary organizational structures can also compromise their ability to control costs. The "tub" model, in which each college keeps the revenue it generates, including tuition, and is responsible for all costs it incurs, reduces central administration's control over resources. While few private institutions are formally organized as tubs, Ehrenberg's research indicates that nearly half operate as such in practice. Adjusting the institutional budgetary models to enhance control over costs could have a considerable effect on tuition increases.

Ehrenberg also encourages colleges and universities to cooperate with competitors via consortia, which promise significant savings. Finally, he exhorts institutions to grow and improve by substitution and by increasing efficiency, not by expansion.

Planning for the Future

Technology and the burgeoning demand for higher and continuing education promise fundamental change for the future of higher education. Managing and directing that change are critical issues that the Forum has engaged for many years.

The vast majority of higher education in this country is provided by nonprofit entities that receive substantial amounts of public funds supporting their efforts. Historically the primary deterrents to private sector entry into higher education have been the huge start-up costs and unprofitability of the traditional university. Today, however, advances in technology and increases in the demand for higher education facilitate focused, low-cost, and profitable private sector entry. In Chapter Six, David Collis considers these primary drivers of change in higher education and recommends strategic responses to them.

Technology can be used in many ways to expand or improve the educational experience. It offers an alternative to learners who cannot afford the time, expense, and relocation disturbance of the traditional four-year undergraduate residential college or university, and it does so at an affordable price. Technology breaks down the traditional rationales for the integration of higher education; by eliminating the need for dormitories and cafeterias, classroom space, and even libraries, technology reduces entry barriers enormously and opens the doors for credible competitors.

While technology is supplanting traditional entry barriers, increases in demand are providing the market opportunity for new entrants. The shift in the composition of demand for higher education from largely eighteen- to twenty-one-year-olds to students over age twenty-five foreshadows a fundamental change in the nature of the industry, inducing new private sector companies to serve the emerging markets. Given this entry path, new companies that build scale and reputation in the older student segment should be able to move into more traditional degree programs, as over time the entrants' attractive price and features will begin to draw younger students as well. Pressure on prices, too, will intensify as it becomes increasingly more difficult to justify large tuition differences between traditional and technology-based degree programs, particularly when some of the less costly programs offer on-line courses taught by the same faculty as the higher priced options.

Collis recommends that colleges and universities respond to the deconstruction of their industry by quickly forming strategic alliances with credible new entrants. Because the supply of good partners is limited, early movers will achieve sustainable advantages—particularly given the winner-take-all higher education market, where the penalty for complacency is high. The biggest mistake established institutions can make, Collis says, is to sit back and see how the market develops, rather than proactively determine the future of their institutions.

Technology promises not only enormous change in the broad structure of the higher education industry but also in the day-to-day conduct of teaching, learning, and research. In Chapter Seven, Michael McRobbie and Judith Palmer describe Indiana University's (IU's) Information Technology Strategic Plan, which outlines its vision for the development, use, and application of information technology (IT) into the next millennium.

Recognizing that the creation of new knowledge and sharing of information are defining features of a university, the goal of IU's strategic plan is to rise to a position of absolute leadership among public universities in the creative use and application of information technology.

The strategic plan recognizes the transformational power of IT and its inevitable and ubiquitous spread in higher education. It emphasizes the speed of technological change, as well as its unpredictability. Two major themes are woven throughout the plan's key recommendations. The first is reliable access for students, faculty, and staff to computing and network services, both on and off the campuses. The second theme is life-cycle replacement funding to allow maintenance of the IT infrastructure at state-of-the-art levels.

McRobbie and Palmer outline strategies to meet the enormous fiscal challenges technology presents. They recommend that any IT strategic plan be accompanied by a business plan estimating expenditures and time horizons to accomplish major objectives. A fiscal analysis should reflect funding priorities for the plan, estimate the costs of each IT activity, and identify possible sources of revenue. In terms of revenue, it is important to consider new and nontraditional funding relationships. These may include partnerships or sponsorships with outside public and private organizations, including the corporate sector.

To address the serious human resource shortage in information technology, the authors suggest a twofold approach. In the short term, higher salaries and greater incentives that more closely parallel those available in the private sector will be necessary. In the long term, in-house training and production of qualified graduates to fill these jobs will help alleviate shortages, although retention likely will remain problematic.

Finally, the authors emphasize that IT strategic plans reflect institutional priorities. Each college and university should thoughtfully consider its IT needs in light of its strengths and mission. On that base, a reasonable and workable plan can be formulated to guide institutions and help them manage the vast transformations that technology brings.

The upheavals wrought on college and university campuses by technological change and the pressures stemming from the need to reduce costs and increase efficiency have come to bear on the workplace in a number of ways. Meanwhile, managers working to direct change and improve systems are faced with an overwhelming variety of strategies and dogmas. In Chapter Eight, Wendell Brase at the University of California, Irvine (UCI), outlines a model for effecting *sustained* improvement.

The empirically based UCI Model for Sustaining Administrative Improvement focuses on the tools that research has shown lead most efficiently and assuredly to improved enterprise performance. Brase's research reveals very strong correlations between managerial behavior patterns and organizational effectiveness. Further statistical analysis suggests a straightforward, multistage causal model; key management behaviors lead to workplace respect, which enables workplace cooperation, which then yields organizational performance.

The data reveal that as few as twenty key management behaviors may provide a strong prediction of workplace respect, forming the base of the improvement model. Further the evidence suggests that these key behaviors are not inborn but can be learned. With the help of management consultants using employee survey results, supervisors were able to show significant improvement across all measured behaviors—including the ones that seem more like traits than acquired skills. These results indicate that important behaviors can be codified, measured, and learned.

The UCI model's simplicity may lead to underestimation of its significance. It demonstrates that there is little a manager can do to influence *directly* workplace cooperation and outcomes; rather, the main role of the effective manager is to foster the behaviors that lead to workplace respect, the linchpin of organizational performance. Any model that fails to focus first on the underlying behaviors of an enterprise also will fail to stimulate long-term, sustainable change.

Conclusion

Traditional colleges and universities today must function in a rapidly changing world, where the rules and conventions that have served them well in the past no longer apply. Technology, a changing competitive environment, and the aging of higher education's growing student body are inexorably shifting the parameters of higher education. Campus leaders can embrace these changes, and guide their institutions into a future that they actively help to shape and influence. Along the way, care should be taken to preserve the fundamental goods and purposes of higher education, so they are not lost in the tides of change sweeping the landscape.

THE AUTHORS

WILLIAM G. BOWEN is president of The Andrew W. Mellon Foundation, a position he has held since 1988. Prior to that, from 1972 to 1988, he was president of Princeton University. From 1967 to 1972, Bill was provost at Princeton, where he was a member of the faculty for thirty years, from 1958 to 1988. Bill has published numerous books and articles. His most recent book, *The Game of Life: College Sports and Educational Values* (2001), was coauthored with James L. Shulman. Other books include *The Shape of the River: Long-Term Consquences of Considering Race in College and University Admissions* (1998), coauthored with Derek Bok; *Universities and Their Leadership* (1998), edited with Harold T. Shapiro; *Inside the Boardroom* (1994); and *In Pursuit of the Ph.D.* (1992), with Neil L. Rudenstine. Bill earned his Ph.D. from Princeton in economics.

WENDELL C. BRASE is vice chancellor for Administrative and Business Services at the University of California, Irvine (UCI). UCI's Administrative and Business Services has been cited with six national awards for process improvement, innovation, and administrative streamlining, including first prize in NACUBO's Higher Education Award Program (1996), Best Practices Award from CAUSE (now EDUCAUSE) (1997), and the RIT/*USA Today* Quality Cup Award (1998). Wendell has twenty-one years of experience in the University of California system. Earlier in his career, he was associate director of the Laboratory for Laser Energetics at the University of Rochester, a laser-fusion project, and assistant director of the Eastman School of Music. He has published several articles in *Planning for Higher Education*, has been a director of the Society for College and University Planning, and is active in NACUBO. Wendell holds two degrees from the Sloan School of Management, Massachusetts Institute of Technology.

DAVID COLLIS is visiting professor of management at the Yale School of Management. Prior to joining Yale, he was associate professor of business administration at Harvard Business School, where he taught for eleven years. In 1996 he was rated the top teacher among all strategy faculty by both MBA students and executives. David's most recent work, with Cynthia Montgomery, is *Creating Corporate Advantage* (Free Press). His other books include *Corporate Strategy: A Resource-Based Approach* (1998) and *Corporate Strategy: Resources and Scope of the Firm* (1997), both also written with Cynthia Montgomery. David has authored numerous articles and book chapters on organizations, competition, strategy, and management and has prepared dozens of Harvard Business School case studies. He serves as a consultant to corporations in the U.S. and the U.K. David earned his Ph.D. in business economics from Harvard.

RONALD G. EHRENBERG is the Irving M. Ives Professor of Industrial and Labor Relations and Economics at Cornell University, the director of the Cornell Higher Education Research Institute, and codirector of Cornell's Institute for Labor Market Policies. He also served for three years as Cornell's vice president for Academic Programs, Planning, and Budgeting. A member of the Cornell faculty for twenty-three years, Ron has authored or coauthored over 100 papers and books. His most recent book is *Tuition Rising: Why College Costs So Much* (2000). Ron is currently a coeditor of the *Journal of Human Resources* and a member of the executive committee of the American Economic Association. He is the editor of *American Universities: National Treasure or Endangered Species?* (Cornell University Press, 1997). Ron earned his Ph.D. in economics from Northwestern University.

JAMES ENGELL is professor of English and Comparative Literature at Harvard University, where he has taught for twenty-one years. He was director of Undergraduate Studies in English and American Literature from 1995 to 1997 and chair of the degree program in History and Literature from 1988 to 1993. He has written numerous books, book chapters, and journal articles. His first book, *The Creative Imagination: Enlightenment to Romanticism* (1981), won the best-first-book prize from Harvard University Press. Jim also received the prize for "outstanding undergraduate instruction amongst the senior faculty" at Harvard in 1995 and the award for excellence and sensitivity in undergraduate teaching at Harvard in 1997. He is currently writing a book about issues in higher education, including the challenges that social and cultural diversity pose to liberal education, and the humanities and their links to the sciences. Jim earned his Ph.D. in English and American Literature from Harvard.

ROBERT H. FRANK is the Goldwin Smith Professor of Economics, Ethics, and Public Policy at Cornell University and professor of economics at Cornell's Johnson Graduate School of Management. He was a Peace Corps volunteer in rural Nepal from 1966 to 1968, chief economist for the Civil Aeronautics Board from 1978 to 1980, and a Fellow at the Center for Advanced Study in the Behavioral Sciences in 1992 to 1993. Bob has written numerous journal articles and books, including *Luxury Fever* (1999), *Passions Within Reason* (1998), *Microeconomics and Behavior* (1991), and *Choosing the Right Pond* (1985). *The Winner-Take-All Society* (1995), coauthored with Philip Cook, was named a Notable Book of the Year by the *New York Times* and was on *Business Week's* list of the ten best books of 1995. Bob's books have been translated into numerous languages, including Chinese, Russian, Portuguese, Spanish, and Italian. He earned his Ph.D. in economics from the University of California, Berkeley.

CAROLINE M. HOXBY is the Morris Kahn Associate Professor of Economics at Harvard University and a Faculty Research Fellow for the National Bureau of Economic Research (NBER). She also is currently the recipient of an Alfred P. Sloan Research Fellowship in Economics and a five-year grant from the National Institute of Child Health and Development. Caroline was a Rhodes Scholar, and her thesis at the University of Oxford was judged the best thesis in economics in 1990. She has written several articles and papers, including "How Teachers' Unions Affect Education Production" (1996), "How the Changing Market Structure of American College Education Explains Tuition" (1997), "Tax Incentives for Higher Education" (1998), and "Explaining Rising Wage and Income Inequality Among the College-Educated," with Bridget Terry (1998). Caroline earned her Ph.D. in economics from the Massachusetts Institute of Technology.

MICHAEL A. MCROBBIE is the vice president for information technology and chief information officer at Indiana University (IU). He also holds several teaching positions, including professor of computer science and professor of philosophy on the Bloomington campus of Indiana University. Michael has been responsible for a major overhaul of the information technology organizations at IU, including their budgets, advisory structure, and security. He also initiated IU's first IT strategic plan, which commenced in late 1998 under his direction. Michael is a member of the Abilene Executive Committee and was recently elected a member of the Internet2 Network Planning and Policy Council. He is the author, coauthor, or editor of a number of books and nearly 100 papers, articles, and reports, and he is on the editorial board of several international journals and book series in informational technology. Michael earned his Ph.D. from the Australian National University.

JUDITH G. PALMER is vice president and chief financial officer of Indiana University, a position she has held for the past five years. From 1991 to 1994, she served as vice president for planning and finance management. Judy is also a part-time associate professor at Indiana's School of Public and Environmental Affairs. Prior to joining Indiana University, Judy was state budget director and fiscal advisor to the governor of Indiana from 1981 to 1985. From 1976 to 1981, she was executive assistant to the governor. She is the chair of the Council on Business Affairs of NASULGC and a member of the Research Universities Council of NACUBO. Judy earned her law degree from Indiana University School of Law, Indianapolis.

JAMES L. SHULMAN is the financial and administrative officer at the Andrew W. Mellon Foundation. He also directs the College and Beyond research project and has program responsibilities for research in higher education and the nonprofit sector. In addition to collaborating on *The Shape of the River: Long-Term Consequences of Considering Race in College and University Admissions* (1998), he has written *The Pale Cast of Thought: Hesitation and Decision in the Renaissance Epic* (1998). His most recent book, *The Game of Life: College Sports and Educational Values* (2001), was co-authored with William G. Bowen.

PART ONE

WINNER-TAKE-ALL MARKETS

CHAPTER ONE

HIGHER EDUCATION: THE ULTIMATE WINNER-TAKE-ALL MARKET?

Robert H. Frank

Frank describes the evolution and effects of the winner-take-all trend in higher education, where success breeds success and failure breeds failure. Pressures from the winner-take-all market have spawned a positional arms race, as universities struggle to maintain and improve their hierarchical rankings. Frank notes the high costs of the positional arms race and its effects on tuition and access to higher education. He argues that collective action by institutions must be permitted to defuse this competition and mitigate the effects of the winner-take-all market.

John Maynard Keynes once compared investing in the stock market to picking the winner of a beauty contest. In each case, it's not who *you* think will win, but who you think *others* will pick. The same characterization increasingly applies to a student's choice among universities. This choice depends much less now on what any individual student may think and much more on what panels of experts think. The annual college ranking issue of *U.S. News & World Report* has become by far the magazine's biggest seller, and the same is true of *Business Week*'s biennial issue ranking the nation's top MBA programs. The size of a school's applicant pool fluctuates sharply in response to even minor movements in these rankings.

In this chapter, I'll discuss some of the reasons for the growing importance of academic rankings. I'll also explore how our increased focus on them has affected the distribution of students and faculty across schools, the distribution of financial aid across students, and the rate at which costs have been escalating in higher education.

The Market for Higher Education

The economist Gordon Winston has said that buyers in the market for higher education confront a decision more like investing in a one-shot cancer cure than shopping for groceries. But this characterization actually understates the difference between the typical market described in economics textbooks and the market for higher education. Shopping for groceries and shopping for a cancer cure in fact have far more in common with one another than with shopping for a spot in an American university.

If popular grocers or oncologists charge inflated fees, their high earnings will attract competitors who will drive prices back down. But that's not the way things work in the market for higher education. There, especially at the high end of the market, demand exceeds supply at the stated price—year in and year out— by an enormous margin. At one small, high-quality liberal arts institution in the East, for example, 4,500 people apply each year for only 500 positions in the freshman class. At universities nearer the pinnacle of the academic pyramid, an even higher proportion of eager customers are routinely turned away.

In contrast, when excess demand arises in the market for an ordinary private good or service, it is almost always fleeting. Thus when Porsche recently introduced its new Boxster, each new delivery was sold out more than a year in advance, yet anyone who really wanted this car could find one at a price. Not so in the upper reaches of the academic market. Despite the persistence of excess demand in this market, universities continue to turn qualified students away, while charging those they admit only about one-third of what it costs to serve them. This pattern, needless to say, bears little resemblance to the one portrayed in economics textbooks.

For present purposes, the salient difference between a university and the producer of a sports car is that, although the attractiveness of a sports car does not depend on the average driving skill level of its buyers, the attractiveness of a university depends strongly on the average intellectual ability of its students. Applicants want to be at a school whose students are accomplished, partly because they can learn more by interacting with such students, but also because that's where the best employers concentrate their recruiting. In short, the university's customers are one of the most important inputs in its production process, and this is not the case for producers of typical private goods and services.

If the ability to affiliate with elite institutions is so highly valued, why don't these institutions simply raise their tuition? The answer is that they need top students every bit as much as top students need them. A school without top-ranked students cannot hope to achieve elite status.

This codependence creates multiple positive feedback loops that amplify the rewards for a university that succeeds in its efforts to move forward in the academic pecking order. And the same positive feedback loops exacerbate the penalties on those who begin to slip in the rankings. When Cornell's Johnson Graduate School of Management jumped from eighteenth to eighth in the *Business Week* rankings in 1998 (the largest such advance in the poll's history), applications for the following year's class rose more than 50 percent. To an extent rivaled perhaps only by the market for trendy nightclubs, higher education is an industry in which success breeds success and failure breeds failure.

Why Does Rank Matter So Much More Now?

Hierarchy in education is nothing new, of course, and it has always been important. But as we are all keenly aware, it has become far more important than in the past. Why this change? The short answer is that the economic reward for elite educational credentials has jumped sharply in recent decades.

Behind this jump lies the spread and intensification of what Philip Cook and I have called "winner-take-all markets." These are markets in which small differences in performance (or even small differences in the credentials used to predict performance) translate into extremely large differences in reward.

Such markets have long been familiar in entertainment and sports. The best soprano may be only marginally better than the second best, but in a world in which most people listen to music on compact discs, there is little need for the second best. In such a world, the best soprano may earn a seven-figure annual salary while the second best struggles to get by. In similar fashion, new technologies allow us to clone the services of the most talented performers in a growing number of occupations, thereby enabling them to serve ever broader and more lucrative markets.

The market for tax advice, for example, was once served almost exclusively by a large army of local practitioners but is increasingly served by the developers of a small handful of software programs. Scores of programs competed for reviewer approval in the early stages of this transition. But once opinion leaders anointed Intuit's TurboTax and Kiplinger's TaxCut as the most comprehensive, user-friendly programs, competing programs faced a nearly impossible task.

A constellation of factors helps us understand why similar shakeouts have occurred in industry after industry. The information revolution has made us more aware of product quality differences than ever and puts us in direct contact with the world's best suppliers. Sharply reduced transportation costs and tariff barriers enable these suppliers to ship their products to us more cheaply than before.

Research and development costs and other fixed costs now comprise a larger share of total costs, making it harder for small producers to achieve efficient scale.

Another important contributor to the winner-take-all trend is that the world's increasingly affluent buyers appear to care more than ever about product rank itself. For example, whereas the demand for any given make of car was once based largely on functional characteristics like size, reliability, and fuel economy, buyers increasingly search for something more. They want a fast car, or one that handles well, or one that stands out from the crowd. These characteristics are far more context dependent than fuel economy and reliability. How fast does a car have to be to impress the potential buyer? If a car produced in 1925 could reach sixty miles per hour *eventually*, the driver would have experienced it as breathtakingly exciting, a *really* fast car. Today if your car does not get from zero to sixty miles per hour in less than six seconds, it doesn't *seem* like a fast car. Context-sensitive characteristics like speed and handling dictate an increasing share of purchase decisions in automobile markets. And when what people want is defined in relative terms, only a limited number of suppliers can deliver. In the extreme case, only a single company can truthfully claim to offer the fastest car in the market.

One result of the movement toward winner-take-all markets has been an explosion in the salaries paid to the handful of key players who are most responsible for an organization's success. American CEOs, for example, earned 419 times as much as the average worker last year, up from only 42 times as much in 1980. The top 1 percent of U.S. earners have seen their real incomes more than double since 1979, a period during which the median income has remained essentially unchanged.

The increase in financial stakes in the business community has spawned an extremely lucrative market for high-end services like business consulting, investment banking, and corporate law—three fields of particular interest in our efforts to understand the increased demand for elite educational credentials. Each field is one in which rank is of paramount importance.

Suppose you were the CEO of a financially distressed corporation and were looking for advice from a management consulting firm. Which firm should you hire, McKinsey—widely thought to be first among equals in the management consulting field—or some lesser ranked firm that is considerably cheaper, yet, in absolute terms, nearly as good? You know that in either case the advice you get may not eliminate your firm's financial woes, and if it doesn't, your board of directors will want to know why. If you had hired McKinsey, you could respond that you sought the best available advice and followed it. Critics might still second-guess you, but you would be far less vulnerable to their charges than if you had hired some lesser ranked firm. And if McKinsey's advice worked, no one would ever complain that you paid too much for it.

The upshot is that McKinsey and a handful of other elite management consulting firms are essentially able to set extremely high prices and still attract more business than they can handle. As employers, such firms also have their pick of the most able college graduates. When they post positions, mail sacks full of résumés arrive in their personnel offices day after day. And no wonder. If a new recruit survives the early rounds and becomes a partner, she'll reap an annual salary of many hundreds of thousands of dollars.

That such salaries persistently attract an enormous surplus of applicants might seem to suggest that the elite consulting firms are paying far too much. Why don't they just offer less money and attract only the number of qualified applicants they need? The answer is not that they have failed to grasp the elementary logic of supply and demand. On the contrary, as in the case of elite universities, they understand that a very different logic governs the hiring decisions of organizations whose fate hinges on reputation and relative performance. These firms need the graduates of elite institutions just as much as those graduates need them. And the more applicants they attract, the better they do.

After all, they are selling advice, perhaps the most difficult of all services to evaluate. They send recruits who are barely out of school to advise seasoned professionals about what they should do with their businesses. Under the circumstances, establishing credibility is a tall order—perhaps an impossibly tall order—for graduates of institutions with less than elite status. When the client knows that he is dealing with a graduate of an elite school, however, things are different. Every year more high school valedictorians apply to Stanford than there are positions in Stanford's freshman class. The client himself may have gone to Stanford in the 1950s, but he knows that if he had applied to Stanford in the last decade, he probably would have been rejected. Although this knowledge may operate completely below the level of conscious awareness, it nonetheless confers an unmistakable gloss on the advice given by the elite school graduate.

For our purposes, the important point is that even if McKinsey and the other elite consulting firms had time to interview everyone who submits an application, they would still have good reasons for confining their attention to the graduates of elite institutions. You might be exceedingly well qualified, but if you are not from one of these schools, odds are they won't even talk to you.

The logic is essentially the same in many other winner-take-all labor markets. Want to be a top mergers-and-acquisitions attorney? Better graduate with honors from an elite law school. Want to be an investment banker? Better go to one of the top-ranked business schools.

One consequence of the growing reward for attending a top-ranked professional or graduate program is that competition for admission into these programs has become much more intense. How can a student assure admission to such a program? In an earlier day, it was sufficient to compile a strong undergraduate record at almost any college or university. But no longer. A friend who teaches at Harvard described to me the case of a woman from a small Florida college who had applied to Harvard's graduate program in economics several years ago. She had scored within a few points of 800 on her GREs, both quantitative and verbal, and also had a very high score on the economics achievement test. She had straight A's and glowing recommendations from several senior professors, who described her as the best student they'd ever encountered. The admissions committee agonized long and hard over this woman's file but in the end decided to reject her. They simply had too many other applicants who had compiled equally strong records at much more highly selective institutions.

Students, in short, confront an increasingly competitive environment. Between 1979 and 1989, the percentage of students who scored above 700 on the SAT verbal section and matriculated at one of the thirty-three "most competitive" schools on the Barron's list rose from 32 percent to 43 percent. And as more and more of the best students attend the most selective schools, the payoff for going to these schools gets ever higher.

The fact that elite schools are increasingly the gateway to professional positions offering six-figure starting salaries has fueled the explosive growth in demand for elite educational credentials. And the growth in demand for elite educational credentials explains the growing importance of academic rankings. The market for higher education, always a winner-take-all market, has become perhaps the quintessential example of such a market.

The Positional Arms Race

Contestants in virtually every winner-take-all market face strong incentives to invest in performance enhancement, thereby to enhance their chances of coming out ahead. As in the classic military arms race, however, many such investments prove mutually offsetting in the end. When each nation spends more on bombs, the balance of power is no different than if none had spent more. Yet that fact alone provides no escape for individual contestants. Countries may find it difficult to spend a lot on bombs, but they find it even more distasteful to be less well armed than their rivals.

In light of the growing importance of rank in the educational marketplace, universities face increasing pressure to bid for the various resources that facilitate the quest for high rank. These pressures have spawned a "positional arms race" that has already proved extremely costly and promises to become more so.

Distinguished, highly visible faculty are one of the key ingredients in the effort to achieve and maintain elite educational status. And so it is no surprise that star faculty command ever higher salaries and require ever more elaborate and costly support. In one well publicized case in 1997, Columbia University offered an annual salary of $300,000 in its effort to lure the Harvard economist Robert Barro to join its faculty. Columbia also offered Barro a large, heavily subsidized apartment near campus; created a high-profile job for his wife; secured a slot in an exclusive Manhattan private school for his son; and offered him the opportunity to hire six colleagues of his own choosing. Barro was sorely tempted by this offer, and indeed he initially accepted it. In the end, however, he apparently could not bring himself to overcome the gravitational pull of Harvard's own high rank.

Top students, as noted, are an essential ingredient of elite educational status, and efforts to attract these students have kept pace with efforts to attract star faculty. Universities and colleges up and down the academic totem pole are spending far more than ever on brochures, videos, mailings, multistate tours by admissions officials, and other efforts to woo top students. Yet when all institutions increase their expenditures on these activities, the effect is similar to an across-the-board increase in advertising by cigarette companies. The additional spending adds to the cost burden but has little impact on the ultimate distribution of consumer choices.

Colleges and universities are spending more now not just to attract good students but also to keep them happy once they arrive. For example, as the material living standards of affluent Americans have escalated in recent years, universities have felt increasing pressure to upgrade campus amenities. Yesterday's double-room occupancy standard in dormitories is giving way to apartment-like suites that house one student per bedroom. Centralized athletic complexes are giving way to in-dorm training facilities that resemble expensive private health clubs. Dining halls are being supplanted by facilities modeled after the food courts in upscale shopping malls. Multimillion-dollar, state-of-the-art classroom facilities are increasingly part of the mix. Universities that fail to offer such facilities often fail in their efforts to attract the disproportionate share of high-achievement students who come from affluent families. But these facilities also create new financial hurdles for middle- and low-income parents.

Career counseling and job placement services are another important focus of the effort to attract top students. In business schools, for example, placement officers are now expected to assure that each MBA student lands not only a prestigious summer internship between the first and second years of study but also the job of his or her choice upon graduation. These demands have proven costly to meet. The staff of the Career Services Office at Cornell's Johnson School, for example, has more than doubled in the last ten years. Changes of this sort in business schools typically portend similar changes in the broader university environment.

If meeting demands for student services is costly, failure to meet these demands often proves even more costly. Student evaluations are one of the two most important components in the *Business Week* rankings formula, and as many top MBA programs have discovered to their chagrin, student dissatisfaction quickly translates into a drop in the rankings.

Implications for Need-Based Financial Aid

The new competitive climate has also produced sweeping changes in financial aid decisions. From the university's perspective, the merit scholar is an asset whose value has appreciated sharply. Other things equal, someone who scored 750 on both sections of the SAT always paid a lower net price at the bursar's window than someone who scored only 700. But never before have we witnessed such intense bidding to attract the highest-scoring students.

Think of yourself as the admissions director of a school trying to move forward in the academic pecking order. On your desk sit the folders for two applicants. They have almost the same credentials, but one is just a little better than the other. She has a 4.2 grade point average while the other has a 3.8. She scored 790 on both SATs, while the other scored only 700. The applicant with better credentials comes from a family with an annual income of $500,000, while the other student's family earns only $30,000. Now, as in the past, you accept both students. In the past, your financial aid package for these students would have been tailored in a way that I think most of us would feel was just: the student from the family with limited means would have gotten a large aid package, and the student with no financial constraints would have gotten a much smaller package, or more likely no aid at all. In today's climate, however, such offers would almost guarantee that the better qualified student would go elsewhere. And that would make your university less attractive to other top students and faculty. In light of the feedback loops discussed earlier, the indirect effects of failure to land even a single top student can multiply manyfold. And this, in a nutshell, explains the growing tendency for merit-based financial aid to displace need-based financial aid.

In sum, universities face increased pressure to pay higher salaries to star faculty, to spend more on marketing, more on student services and amenities, and more on financial aid to top-ranked students. It is little wonder, then, that their financial situations have grown more precarious, despite the record growth in the value of their endowment portfolios.

Positional Arms Control Agreements

Unlike expenditures on military armaments, not all expenditures in the battle for elite educational status are socially wasteful. Conveniently located workout rooms are better than distant ones, for example, and marketing expenditures in some instances may facilitate an improved match between students and schools. But the competitive dynamics that govern these expenditures virtually guarantee a measure of social waste. In the realm of marketing, for example, the socially optimal allocation would be to increase marketing expenditures until the social value of the improved match quality thus obtained was exactly equal to its cost. Individual universities have powerful incentives to push marketing expenditures past that point, however, because each dollar they spend creates the additional private benefit of helping lure a good student away from another university. The rub is that these private benefits sum to zero on the social scale, since one school's gain is offset by another's loss. From a social perspective, then, it would be better if all schools spent less. Yet no school dares cut its own expenditures unilaterally, just as no nation dares reduce its spending on armaments unilaterally.

Under these circumstances, it is often possible to generate socially preferred outcomes through what I call "positional arms control" agreements, pacts in which contestants pledge mutual restraint. Many elite institutions, for example, were once party to an agreement whereby they pledged to target limited financial aid money for those students with the greatest financial needs. This was essentially a cartel agreement to curb competition for students with elite credentials. Animated by its belief that unbridled competition always and everywhere leads to the best outcome, the Justice Department took a dim view of this agreement and brought an antitrust suit that led to its termination.

Once we appreciate the logic of the financial incentives that confront participants in winner-take-all markets, however, we may feel less inclined to embrace the mantra that all outcomes of open competition must be good. The problem, as noted, is that when reward depends on rank, behavior that looks attractive to each individual often looks profoundly unattractive from the perspective of the group. Collusive agreements to restrain these behaviors can create gains for everyone. Of course, cooperative agreements to limit competition can also cause harm, as in the notorious price-fixing cases of antitrust lore.

The challenge, of course, is to make informed distinctions. Antitrust authorities might consider a retreat from their uncritical belief that unlimited competition necessarily leads to the greatest good for all. Manifestly it does not. Collective agreements should be scrutinized not on quasi-religious grounds but according to the practical test of whether they limit harmful effects of competition without compromising its many benign effects. In my view, the collective agreement among universities regarding financial aid policy was a positional arms control agreement that clearly met this test.

Looking Ahead

In New York state in 1997 the ninetieth-percentile earner earned twenty times as much as the tenth-percentile earner, the highest value of this ratio for any state and the highest in New York's history. In Utah in the same year the ninetieth-percentile earner earned only seven times as much as the tenth-percentile earner. The economic forces that give rise to winner-take-all markets are here to stay. Years hence, the ratio in New York will be still higher than it is today, and the ratio in Utah will be much closer to the ratio in New York. As the top jobs in society grow ever more lucrative, competition to land those jobs will grow steadily more intense, as will the competition for the educational credentials that are increasingly the prerequisite for landing even an initial interview.

No university, acting alone, can escape the powerful logic of the positional arms race. Yet there remain compelling ethical reasons both for limiting the escalation in the cost of acquiring higher education and for basing financial aid more heavily on need than on merit. Indeed, the growth in income and wealth inequality caused by spreading winner-take-all markets makes the case for cost containment and need-based aid more compelling than ever. But such goals can be met only through collective action. Positional arms control agreements may be the only practical way to keep higher education within reach for the average American family. To resist such agreements on the grounds that they are anticompetitive would make sense only if the market for higher education were just like the market for an ordinary private good or service.

CHAPTER TWO

THE RETURN TO ATTENDING A MORE SELECTIVE COLLEGE: 1960 TO THE PRESENT

Caroline M. Hoxby

Hoxby considers the monetary return associated with graduation from selective institutions, based on estimating the lifetime earnings of graduates of various colleges compared to the costs of attending those colleges. Her results show that across the entire spectrum of colleges, people who invest in education earn back their investment several times over during their careers. When earnings are corrected for differences in aptitude—that is, when two graduates with the same measured aptitude are compared—graduates from selective colleges still tend to earn more over their careers.

Every year families are faced with deciding whether a child who has been admitted to several colleges should attend a more selective, more expensive college or a less selective, less expensive college. This chapter offers empirical evidence relevant to that decision—specifically, estimates of the returns to investing in a more selective college. In order to establish trends in these returns over time, I make calculations for people who entered college in 1960, 1972, and 1982. I also project returns for students who are entering college now. I estimate returns two ways: controlling and not controlling for a student's own measured college aptitude. The estimates that control for aptitude would be relevant to a student who has already been admitted to colleges and is trying to choose among them. The estimates that do not control for aptitude would be relevant to a high school student trying to decide whether to increase his study effort in order to gain admission to a more selective college.

Computing the return to education is a standard problem in labor economics, and, at least in theory, computing the return to attending a more selective college is particularly simple. The prospective student only needs to consider his costs of attending various colleges and his lifetime earnings conditional on attending various colleges. In the literature on returns to education, there is general agreement that the return to education has been increasing since the early 1970s. There is also general agreement that the return to education has been increasing more for people of higher measured aptitude.[1] To some extent, these trends are external to American colleges due to a change in the environment, probably caused by changes in technology and international trade. We should not be surprised to find such external forces affecting the return to graduating from a more selective college, but they would not necessarily do so. There is reason to think, however, that selective colleges are partially responsible for the fact that the return to education has been increasing more for people of higher measured aptitude.

In other work, I have shown that, from 1940 to the present, the market for college education has become significantly more integrated (Hoxby, 1997a, 1997b). That is, students have become more mobile geographically and better informed about how their own aptitude fits into the national distribution, their college options, and financial aid opportunities. Colleges, symmetrically, have become better informed about the aptitude and finances of students from nonlocal high schools. The growing integration of the market has generated colleges that are more specialized in educating students of a certain type. For instance, I have shown that the distribution of SAT scores within each college has narrowed, and the overlap in SAT scores between colleges has diminished. Market integration has also generated a stronger correlation between the inputs that a college offers (the costliness of its faculty, facilities, and so on) and the aptitude of the student body it attracts. Colleges' policies about tuition and subsidies (a general term that embraces all forms of institutional aid) are increasingly constrained by market forces—that is, by the reaction of students. In this environment, we expect to find changes in the return to attending a more selective college.

In this chapter, I consider only the monetary costs of and returns to attending a more selective college, although collegiate education naturally generates nonmonetary benefits. In addition, I focus on private costs and returns, not social costs and returns. In this context, the word *private* refers to the personal nature of the costs and returns, not the control of the college. The difference between private and social costs is particularly important for students choosing between publicly controlled and privately controlled colleges. A student considers only the tuition she herself paid when calculating her private costs, but social costs would include the tax burden she imposes on other people if she chooses to attend a public college.

In keeping to the question that opens the chapter, I focus on baccalaureate-granting colleges that have at least minimal selectivity. This means that I do not analyze the large number of American colleges that are nonselective, in the sense that they admit any student who has a high school diploma and can demonstrate basic readiness for college. Furthermore, I focus on people who actually attain the baccalaureate degree, not on the decision to attend college at all or the decision to persist in college. Elsewhere, there is useful research on nonselective colleges, two-year colleges, and the decisions to attend and persist in college.[2]

The Student's Problem

Consider a student calculating monetary returns to graduating from two alternative colleges to which he has been admitted. To keep the problem simple, let us assume that he will attend full time and graduate with a baccalaureate degree after four years. There are only a few components to the student's calculation because many of the opportunity costs associated with attending college, such as the income he could earn if he worked instead of going to college, will not depend on which college he chooses.[3] He needs to know the present value of his total cost of attending each college, taking into account its tuition, fees, and any financial aid that has been offered to him. For instance, the student would compare:

$$Present\ Discounted\ Cost\ of\ College\ A = \sum_{t=1}^{t=4} \frac{\left(tuition^A_{it} + fees^A_{it} - institutional\ grants^A_{ix}\right)}{(1 + \delta)^{t-1}}$$

to

$$Present\ Discounted\ Cost\ of\ College\ B = \sum_{t=1}^{t=4} \frac{\left(tuition^B_{it} + fees^B_{it} - institutional\ grants^B_{ix}\right)}{(1 + \delta)^{t-1}}\ [4]$$

The most a student can pay is typically the sum of four years of full tuition and fees, but the average student pays less. Below I show calculations for both full tuition and average tuition paid. The costs shown above have been discounted back to the year in which the student makes his decision. In the empirical work that follows, all calculations are in real (inflation adjusted) dollars, so the appropriate discount rate is a real discount rate (the intrinsic value a person puts on consuming this year versus next year)—a number generally accepted to be between 0 percent and 3 percent.

The student also needs to consider the stream of earnings associated with attending each of the two colleges. Of course, only part of a person's future earnings depends on his college choice. Much depends on his aptitude and the education he has already received in primary and secondary school. Career incomes from the two colleges are the presented discounted sums of annual earnings:

$$Career\ Discounted\ Earnings\ Associated\ with\ College\ A = \sum_{t=5}^{t=38} \frac{Earnings_{it}^A}{(1 + \delta)^{t-1}}$$

and

$$Career\ Discounted\ Earnings\ Associated\ with\ College\ B = \sum_{t=5}^{t=38} \frac{Earnings_{it}^B}{(1 + \delta)^{t-1}} \quad 5$$

Earnings are subscripted with the letter i to remind us that an individual's earnings do not just depend on his college; they also depend on his individual traits. In other words, we will need to account for individual aptitude if we are to simulate students' opportunities accurately. Accounting for the effects of individual aptitude on earnings is a well-known and only partly remediable problem. In this chapter, I am able to control for some of the key measures of aptitude that colleges use to admit students: individuals' college admission test scores, high school grades, and other high school standardized test scores.

The Data

In order to compute the return to graduating from a more selective college, it is necessary to have data on income, college attendance, aptitude, and family background for a nationally representative sample of individuals. Such data must be matched to institutional information on colleges, such as tuition and selectivity. In practice, these data requirements can be fulfilled by only a few surveys, all of which are used in this chapter. The surveys used are, in chronological order, *Occupational Changes in a Generation* (a supplement to the 1973 *Current Population Survey*), the *National Longitudinal Study of the Class of 1972* (Center for Human Resource Research, 1986), and the *National Longitudinal Survey of Youth* (Center for Human Resource Research, 1997). These surveys are described in detail in Hoxby and Terry (1998). For this chapter, it is only necessary to know that the three surveys provide us with information on people who entered college in 1960, 1972, and 1982. The years of college entry are approximate, since people who started college one or two years off-schedule are included.

To estimate career income, I use individuals' incomes at age thirty-two. Thirty-two is old enough for earnings patterns to be established and young enough to give us reasonably current earnings patterns.[6] I focus on the earnings of men because comparing their earnings over time is straightforward. Women, in contrast, have changed their working and childbearing behavior significantly over the period of interest, making comparisons difficult. Fortunately, focusing on males does not pose a problem for contemporary females seeking evidence to guide their college choices. A female student who is about to enter a selective college in 1998 can use recent men's earnings to get a reasonable prediction of her own returns.

Colleges are divided into eight rank groups, based on Barron's rating of their selectivity in *Barron's Profiles of American Colleges*. It is possible to use a finer ranking of colleges (see Hoxby and Terry, 1998), but the precision of earnings estimates falls as the ranking becomes finer. The Barron's index has two additional merits: it is widely accepted and its construction is external to this chapter (it does not take returns or costs into account). Table 2.1a lists the colleges in each of the top four rank groups and describes the colleges in the each of the next four rank groups. Nonselective colleges are omitted because the thought experiment in this chapter involves students who have expressed at least some interest in selective colleges.

The Background: College Selectivity and Tuition

Table 2.1b presents average SAT scores for each college rank group in 1960, 1972, 1982, and 1996. Scores have been converted into percentile scores using the national distribution of SAT scores in the relevant years. This conversion is useful for making comparisons over long periods of time because the distribution of SAT scores has shifted down over time.[7] Since the verbal and mathematics tests have different typical distributions (the verbal test is significantly more discriminating among high scorers), the conversion also aids comparison across the tests. Finally, the conversion is almost a necessity for comparing colleges of widely differing selectivity. The reason is that a 100 point difference near the top of the test score range (between 700 and 800 on an individual test) corresponds to only a few percentiles in the national distribution, but a 100 point difference near the middle of the range (between 450 and 550 on an individual test) corresponds to almost 30 percentiles.[8]

The table demonstrates, first, that Barron's ranking does indeed reflect measured college aptitude and, second, that colleges in the top-rank groups have grown more selective over time. Average aptitude in colleges that have minimal selectivity (rank group 8) has fallen over time, as has aptitude in nonselective colleges, which are not shown in the table.[9] These changes reflect the more general increase in the tendency of students to be sorted among colleges on the basis of aptitude.[10] I separate public and private colleges in the table because the public-private

TABLE 2.1A.   COLLEGES BY BARRON'S SELECTIVITY INDEX

COLLEGES IN RANK GROUP 1 (MOST COMPETITIVE)
Amherst College, Bowdoin College, Brown University, California Institute of
Technology, Harvey Mudd College, Pomona College, Columbia College of
Columbia University, Cooper Union, Cornell College of Cornell University (private),
Dartmouth College, Harvard University, Haverford College, Johns Hopkins
University, Massachusetts Institute of Technology, Mount Holyoke College,
Princeton University, Rice University, Smith College, Stanford University,
Swarthmore College, University of Pennsylvania, Wellesley College, Williams
College, Yale University.

COLLEGES IN RANK GROUP 2 (HIGHLY COMPETITIVE PLUS)
Bennington College, Carnegie-Mellon University, Colgate University,
Colorado School of Mines, Barnard College, Northwestern University, Reed College,
Rose-Hulman Institute of Technology, St. John's College (Maryland), Tufts
University, University of California-Berkeley, University of Chicago.

COLLEGES IN RANK GROUP 3 (HIGHLY COMPETITIVE)
Bates College, Brandeis University, Bucknell University, Carleton College, Case
Western Reserve University, Colby College, College of William and Mary, Colorado
College, Davidson College, Duke University, Franklin and Marshall Colleges,
Georgetown University, Georgia Institute of Technology, Grinnell College, Hamilton
College, Kalamazoo College, Kenyon College, Lafayette College, Lehigh University,
Middlebury College, New College of the University of South Florida, Oberlin
College, Occidental College, Polytechnic Institute of New York, Rensselaer
Polytechnic Institute, St. John's College (New Mexico), St. Olaf's College, Stevens
Institute of Technology, Trinity College, Union College, University of Dallas,
University of Notre Dame, University of Rochester, University of the South,
University of Virginia, Vassar College, Washington University.

COLLEGES IN RANK GROUP 4 (VERY COMPETITIVE PLUS)
Bard College, Pitzer College, Scripps College, Clark University, Clarkson College of
Technology, Coe College, College of the Atlantic, Connecticut College, Emory
University, Gustavus Adolphus College, Hampshire College, Illinois Institute of
Technology, St. Lawrence University, University of California-Santa Barbara,
University of Michigan (Ann Arbor campus), Vanderbilt University, Washington and
Lee University.

COLLEGES IN RANK GROUP 5 (VERY COMPETITIVE)
Colleges in this category consider applicants who have grade point averages of
B– at least and who rank in the top 50 percent of their graduating class. These
colleges typically report median SAT scores between 525 and 575.

COLLEGES IN RANK GROUP 6 (COMPETITIVE PLUS)
Colleges in this category consider applicants who have grade point averages of
B– at least and who rank in the top 67 percent of their graduating class. These
colleges typically report median SAT scores between 500 and 525.

(continued)

TABLE 2.1A   (*continued*)

COLLEGES IN RANK GROUP 7 (COMPETITIVE)
Colleges in this category consider applicants who have grade point averages of C+
at least and who rank in the top 67 percent of their graduating class. These colleges
typically report median SAT scores between 425 and 500.

COLLEGES IN RANK GROUP 8 (LESS COMPETITIVE)
Colleges in this category consider applicants who have grade point averages of C at
least and who rank in the top 75 percent of their graduating class. These colleges
typically report median SAT scores below 425.

*The remaining colleges in the United States are considered noncompetitive or
nonselective.* These colleges admit many of the students with SAT scores in the
lower tail of the distribution.

Specialized colleges (art schools, music schools, U.S. military academies) are not
included in the analysis.

Source: The index is taken from the 1980 Barron's "College Admissions Selector," which also contains the names of the colleges in rank groups 5 through 8. The year 1980 was chosen to cor-
respond with the statistics that follow throughout this chapter. The index has changed so little
in recent years, however, that none of the statistics would be significantly altered if the 1996
index were used.

distinction will be useful for considering tuition differences. At this point, it is worth
noting that there are no publicly controlled colleges in rank group 1.[11]

Tables 2.2a and 2.2b show several measures of college tuition, by rank group,
for 1960, 1972, 1982, and 1997. Because people in the three surveys described
above entered college in 1960, 1972, and 1982, these three years are the base years
that I use to calculate the returns to investing in a more selective college education.
Table 2.2a shows tuition in dollars of the day; Table 2.2b shows inflation-adjusted
tuition in 1997 dollars. Comparing tuition over time can be deceptive if it is
measured in dollars of the day.[12] For private colleges, I show both full tuition and
average tuition paid. A public college typically charges lower tuition to students
who reside in the state that financially supports the college. Thus for public colleges, I show both in-state and out-of-state tuition, as well as average tuition paid.

Tables 2.2a and 2.2b demonstrate that more selective colleges tend to charge
higher tuition, regardless of whether we examine full tuition or average tuition
paid. One exception to this rule are private colleges in rank group 1, which have
lower tuition paid than colleges in rank group 2. Also departing from this rule are
the public colleges in rank groups 2 and 3, which have lower in-state tuition than
public colleges in rank group 4. It would be a mistake to make too much of this
departure since it depends on the policies of just a few colleges.[13] Tables 2.2a and
2.2b also show that, although the tuition increase for moving from a rank group 8

TABLE 2.1B.   AVERAGE SAT SCORES, BY COLLEGE SELECTIVITY

Scores are converted into national percentile scores to facilitate comparison across years, tests, and colleges.

| | Verbal Scores | | | | | | | |
| | Private Colleges | | | | Public Colleges | | | |
	1960	1972	1982	1996	1960	1972	1982	1996
Rank 1 Colleges	92	95	95	96	nc	nc	nc	nc
Rank 2 Colleges	86	92	92	93	78	80	83	84
Rank 3 Colleges	85	90	90	90	79	87	89	84
Rank 4 Colleges	79	84	86	86	79	84	79	77
Rank 5 Colleges	77	83	81	81	69	79	79	77
Rank 6 Colleges	69	75	79	78	49	58	70	68
Rank 7 Colleges	57	64	62	61	50	62	60	57
Rank 8 Colleges	41	39	37	35	39	36	30	28

Nonselective or noncompetitive colleges absorb the remainder of the SAT score distribution.

| | Math Scores | | | | | | | |
| | Private Colleges | | | | Public Colleges | | | |
	1960	1972	1982	1996	1960	1972	1982	1996
Rank 1 Colleges	89	91	92	93	nc*	nc	nc	nc
Rank 2 Colleges	79	85	88	89	78	81	87	88
Rank 3 Colleges	80	86	86	86	77	84	88	88
Rank 4 Colleges	74	77	77	77	77	77	77	76
Rank 5 Colleges	67	75	73	74	62	71	74	74
Rank 6 Colleges	60	66	66	66	52	52	64	64
Rank 7 Colleges	51	53	52	49	46	52	52	49
Rank 8 Colleges	34	31	29	27	23	23	23	23

Nonselective or noncompetitive colleges absorb the remainder of the SAT score distribution.

The abbreviation *nc* indicates that there are no public colleges in the rank 1 group.

TABLE 2.2A. AVERAGE COLLEGE TUITION IN DOLLARS OF THE DAY, BY COLLEGE SELECTIVITY

Private Colleges

	Full Tuition				*Average Tuition Paid*		
	1960	1972	1982	1997	1972	1982	1995
Rank 1	$1,262	$2,837	$6,384	$19,885	$2,242	$6,001	$16,439
Rank 2	$1,100	$2,749	$6,312	$20,833	$2,587	$6,419	$18,582
Rank 3	$1,051	$2,637	$5,990	$21,065	$2,162	$5,593	$17,583
Rank 4	$ 993	$2,584	$5,739	$20,113	$2,190	$5,439	$15,839
Rank 5	$ 835	$2,306	$4,895	$17,532	$1,939	$4,702	$13,912
Rank 6	$ 702	$2,059	$4,491	$15,251	$1,695	$3,947	$11,675
Rank 7	$ 626	$1,813	$3,753	$12,632	$1,549	$3,285	$ 9,131
Rank 8	$ 456	$1,391	$2,950	$ 9,414	$1,232	$2,638	$ 6,735

Public Colleges

	Tuition for In-State Students				*Tuition for Out-of-State Students*				*Average Tuition Paid*		
	1960	1972	1982	1997	1960	1972	1982	1997	1972	1982	1995
Rank 1	nc	nc	nc	nc	nc	nc	nc	nc	nc	nc	nc
Rank 2	$ 94	$595	$1,277	$4,684	$501	$2,004	$4,465	$13,907	$818	$2,438	$6,411
Rank 3	$176	$567	$1,029	$4,241	$498	$1,324	$2,481	$13,353	$745	$1,239	$5,234
Rank 4	$250	$645	$1,322	$4,098	$600	$2,135	$4,430	$13,082	$671	$2,194	$4,598
Rank 5	$276	$683	$1,157	$4,019	$517	$1,604	$2,821	$11,146	$579	$1,342	$4,836
Rank 6	$160	$527	$1,010	$3,562	$432	$1,405	$2,719	$ 9,531	$496	$1,064	$3,679
Rank 7	$145	$518	$ 950	$3,244	$361	$1,308	$2,424	$ 8,764	$458	$ 966	$3,085
Rank 8	$101	$422	$ 749	$2,439	$284	$1,086	$1,885	$ 6,612	$366	$ 722	$2,236

For private colleges, average tuition paid is approximately equal to tuition minus average institutional aid. The abbreviation *nc* indicates that there are no public colleges in the rank 1 group. Measures of average tuition paid are not available for 1960 or after 1995.

TABLE 2.2B.   AVERAGE COLLEGE TUITION IN 1997 DOLLARS, BY COLLEGE SELECTIVITY

Private Colleges

	Full Tuition				Average Tuition Paid		
	1960	1972	1982	1997	1972	1982	1995
Rank 1	$3,865	$7,615	$8,567	$19,885	$6,018	$8,054	$16,625
Rank 2	$3,369	$7,378	$8,471	$20,833	$6,944	$8,614	$18,793
Rank 3	$3,220	$7,078	$8,039	$21,065	$5,803	$7,506	$17,782
Rank 4	$3,042	$6,935	$7,701	$20,113	$5,878	$7,299	$16,018
Rank 5	$2,559	$6,189	$6,569	$17,532	$5,204	$6,311	$14,069
Rank 6	$2,150	$5,526	$6,027	$15,251	$4,549	$5,296	$11,807
Rank 7	$1,917	$4,866	$5,037	$12,632	$4,158	$4,409	$ 9,234
Rank 8	$1,398	$3,733	$3,958	$ 9,414	$3,307	$3,540	$ 6,811

Public Colleges

	Tuition for In-State Students				Tuition for Out-of-State Students				Average Tuition Paid		
	1960	1972	1982	1997	1960	1972	1982	1997	1972	1982	1995
Rank 1	nc	nc	nc	nc	nc	nc	nc	nc	nc	nc	nc
Rank 2	$286	$1,597	$1,714	$4,684	$1,535	$5,379	$5,992	$13,907	$2,196	$3,272	$6,484
Rank 3	$538	$1,522	$1,381	$4,241	$1,524	$3,554	$3,330	$13,353	$2,000	$1,663	$5,293
Rank 4	$766	$1,731	$1,774	$4,098	$1,838	$5,730	$5,945	$13,082	$1,801	$2,944	$4,650
Rank 5	$847	$1,833	$1,552	$4,019	$1,583	$4,305	$3,785	$11,146	$1,554	$1,801	$4,891
Rank 6	$490	$1,414	$1,356	$3,562	$1,322	$3,771	$3,648	$ 9,531	$1,331	$1,428	$3,721
Rank 7	$444	$1,390	$1,274	$3,244	$1,105	$3,511	$3,253	$ 8,764	$1,229	$1,296	$3,120
Rank 8	$309	$1,133	$1,005	$2,439	$ 870	$2,915	$2,530	$ 6,612	$ 982	$ 969	$2,261

The abbreviation *nc* indicates that there are no public colleges in the rank 1 group. Measures of average tuition paid are not available for 1960 or after 1995. The price deflator used for putting dollars of the day into 1997 dollars is the consumer durable goods price index.

to a rank group 5 private college is large, the tuition increase for moving from a rank group 4 to a rank group 1 private college is small. For instance, examining Table 2.2b, we see that the tuition difference between rank groups 1 and 4 was between $700 and $900 in all three years.

Table 2.2b also shows that average college tuition has risen over time, in real terms, for selective colleges. The rise in college tuition is widely recognized, and it has been analyzed elsewhere.[14] It is worth noting, however, that the increase in tuition is sometimes exaggerated in the popular press by (1) using dollars of the day rather than real dollars, (2) showing full tuition rather than average tuition paid, and (3) comparing colleges of different selectivity (or an individual college that has significantly raised its selectivity over time).

Earnings and Costs Associated with More Selective Colleges

In this section, I show earnings of men who graduate from colleges of differing selectivity, and I present estimates of their lifetime earnings. I compare the differences in lifetime earnings to the differences in total college costs. I do not control for the effects of individual aptitude on earnings—I reserve that exercise for the next section. The results presented in this section are, nevertheless, useful. There is considerable interest in income differences by college rank, regardless of the fact that some of the differences reflect aptitude differences. Also, the results of this section would be the information one would give to a high school student who had the opportunity to improve his college aptitude through increased study effort. Finally, this section illustrates the exercise in a simple form and, thus, provides a good introduction to the more complicated version of the exercise that attempts to account for aptitude.

Table 2.3 shows the average income at age thirty-two of a baccalaureate-holding male, by college rank group. The men who entered college around 1960 were age thirty-two in 1972, those who entered college around 1972 were age thirty-two in 1986, and those who entered around 1982 were age thirty-two in 1994 or 1995. The first panel of the table shows incomes in dollars of the day; the second panel shows incomes in inflation-adjusted 1997 dollars. In the top two rank groups, the incomes reported are close to actual *median* incomes rather than *mean* incomes owing to survey "topcoding," the censoring of reported incomes of high earners. The topcoding should not be considered a problem—it simply means that the analysis is appropriate for predicting the returns of a fairly typical student.[15]

Table 2.3 shows that men who graduate from more selective colleges tend to earn substantially more by age thirty-two than men who graduate from less selective colleges. Moreover, the income differences between rank groups have been

TABLE 2.3.   AVERAGE INCOME AT AGE THIRTY-TWO, BY COLLEGE SELECTIVITY

in Dollars of the Day

	Men Who Entered College in 1960		Men Who Entered College in 1972		Men Who Entered College in 1982	
	Private Colleges	Public Colleges	Private Colleges	Public Colleges	Private Colleges	Public Colleges
Rank 1 Colleges	$19,648	nc	$42,943	nc	$57,135	nc
Rank 2 Colleges	$18,987	$18,420	$35,992	$33,453	$51,200	$47,631
Rank 3 Colleges	$19,014	$18,266	$35,864	$33,222	$49,263	$45,011
Rank 4 Colleges	$18,555	$17,301	$35,084	$32,116	$47,500	$42,500
Rank 5 Colleges	$18,223	$16,881	$34,929	$32,049	$46,837	$39,373
Rank 6 Colleges	$16,327	$14,753	$34,381	$31,925	$41,176	$37,085
Rank 7 Colleges	$15,733	$14,703	$33,039	$31,138	$38,449	$35,568
Rank 8 Colleges	$11,792	$12,811	$27,735	$28,601	$34,459	$33,660

in 1997 Dollars

	Men Who Entered College in 1960		Men Who Entered College in 1972		Men Who Entered College in 1982	
	Private Colleges	Public Colleges	Private Colleges	Public Colleges	Private Colleges	Public Colleges
Rank 1 Colleges	$52,735	nc	$52,920	nc	$58,556	nc
Rank 2 Colleges	$50,961	$49,439	$44,354	$41,225	$52,473	$48,815
Rank 3 Colleges	$51,034	$49,026	$44,196	$40,940	$50,488	$46,130
Rank 4 Colleges	$49,802	$46,436	$43,235	$39,577	$48,681	$43,557
Rank 5 Colleges	$48,911	$45,309	$43,044	$39,495	$48,002	$40,352
Rank 6 Colleges	$43,822	$39,597	$42,369	$39,342	$42,200	$38,007
Rank 7 Colleges	$42,227	$39,463	$40,715	$38,372	$39,405	$36,453
Rank 8 Colleges	$31,650	$34,385	$34,178	$35,246	$35,316	$34,497

The calculations are based on men who hold at least a baccalaureate degree and are respondents in the *Occupational Changes in a Generation* survey (1960 college entrants), *National Longitudinal Survey of the Class of 1972* (1972 college entrants), or the *National Longitudinal Survey of Youth* (1983 college entrants). The average incomes are calculated using survey weights so that they are nationally representative. The abbreviation *nc* indicates that there are no public colleges in the rank 1 group. The price deflator used for putting dollars of the day into 1997 dollars is the consumer durable goods price index.

growing over time for post-1972 college entrants. For instance, there is a 55 percent income difference between men who entered rank 1 and rank 8 private colleges in 1972. The corresponding income difference for men who entered college in 1982 is 66 percent. The growth in income differences between rank groups is particularly large for more selective colleges. There was a 6 percent income difference between men who entered rank 1 and rank 4 private colleges in 1960, but the corresponding income difference for men who entered college in 1972 or 1982 was about 20 percent.

Table 2.4 shows the results of using income at age thirty-two to estimate career incomes. I formed the estimates using empirical age-earnings profiles from two large wage surveys, the *Current Population Survey* and the *Panel Survey of Income Dynamics*. There is an appropriate estimation method for each of these surveys, which can be described briefly as follows. I use *Current Population Survey* data to estimate the relationship, at a given point in time, between the incomes of thirty-two-year-olds and the incomes of similar people who are older and younger. I use *Panel Survey of Income Dynamics* data to estimate the relationship of a thirty-two-year-old's income to his own previous income and his own later income. Appendix A

TABLE 2.4. CAREER INCOME BY COLLEGE SELECTIVITY, 1997 DOLLARS

	Not Corrected for College Aptitude					
	Men Who Entered College in 1960		*Men Who Entered College in 1972*		*Men Who Entered College in 1982*	
	Private Colleges	**Public Colleges**	**Private Colleges**	**Public Colleges**	**Private Colleges**	**Public Colleges**
Rank 1 Colleges	$2,615,634	nc	$2,624,782	nc	$2,904,332	nc
Rank 2 Colleges	$2,527,639	$2,452,158	$2,199,919	$2,044,730	$2,602,639	$2,421,218
Rank 3 Colleges	$2,531,234	$2,431,655	$2,192,096	$2,030,611	$2,504,177	$2,288,037
Rank 4 Colleges	$2,470,130	$2,303,190	$2,144,421	$1,963,008	$2,414,559	$2,160,393
Rank 5 Colleges	$2,425,932	$2,247,278	$2,134,947	$1,958,913	$2,380,857	$2,001,439
Rank 6 Colleges	$2,173,528	$1,963,990	$2,101,450	$1,951,333	$2,093,092	$1,885,134
Rank 7 Colleges	$2,094,452	$1,957,333	$2,019,425	$1,903,230	$1,954,471	$1,808,021
Rank 8 Colleges	$1,569,806	$1,705,460	$1,695,232	$1,748,164	$1,751,647	$1,711,033

Estimates are based on a working life of thirty-four years and a 0 percent real discount rate. Career income estimates are based on the age-earnings profile in the 1995 *Current Population Survey.* Career income estimates for top-ranked colleges are underestimated owing to topcoding (censoring of high incomes) and the method used to estimate career income (see Appendix A). The abbreviation *nc* indicates that there are no public colleges in the rank 1 group. Approximate estimates for a 3 percent real discount rate may be computed by multiplying the numbers in the table by 0.5. The price deflator used for putting dollars of the day into 1997 dollars is the consumer durable goods price index.

describes the two methods in detail. They produce similar results. The appendix also explains why both methods tend to *understate* the incomes of graduates of highly selective colleges, especially for recent years. Readers should be aware that the differences between the career earnings of graduates of more and less selective colleges are systemically understated, especially for men who entered college in 1982.

The estimates in Table 2.4 were computed under the assumption that people work thirty-four years (age twenty-two to age sixty-five or age twenty-seven to age seventy, for example) and do not discount the future. These assumptions are relatively innocuous because they can be easily relaxed. For instance, if a person discounts the future at 3 percent per year (a high real discount rate), he should multiply the numbers in the table by about 0.5.[16]

Table 2.4 shows that men who graduate from more selective colleges tend to earn substantially more over their careers than men who graduate from less selective colleges. A typical man who entered a rank 1 private college in 1982 can expect to earn about $2.9 million over his career, while a man who entered a rank 8 private college at the same time can expect to earn about $1.75 million over his career. Note that these are *real 1997 dollars*—inflation makes observed career incomes appear to be larger. Among 1982 college entrants, the career income difference between the typical rank 1 and rank 3 graduate is $400,000. It is also worth noting that career income differences by college rank are growing over time, especially for men who entered college after 1972 or entered colleges in rank 5 and above.

It is obvious that the career income differences just described swamp the differences in the total costs of attending more versus less selective colleges. In Table 2.5, I make this point more precisely by examining students who attend colleges that are two selectivity levels apart. A difference of two selectivity levels is large enough to be interesting but small enough to be a plausible thought experiment. Table 2.5 shows the ratio of the earnings difference to the cost difference for a move of two selectivity levels. For instance, the numbers in the first column are

$$\frac{(career\ income\ associated\ with\ rank\ 1\ college) - (career\ income\ associated\ with\ rank\ 3\ college)}{(4\ years\ tuition\ in\ rank\ 1\ college) - (4\ years\ tuition\ in\ rank\ 3\ college)}$$

for men who entered private colleges in 1960. The left section of Table 2.5 considers moving from a private college to another, more selective private college. The right section considers moving from a public college to a more selective private college. The top section of Table 2.5 assumes that students pay full tuition at private colleges and in-state tuition at public colleges. The bottom section assumes that student pay the average tuition paid at both private and public colleges.

TABLE 2.5.   RATIO OF EARNINGS DIFFERENCE TO COST DIFFERENCE ASSOCIATED WITH MOVING UP TWO SELECTIVITY LEVELS

Not Corrected for College Aptitude

$$Ratio = \frac{Increase\ in\ Career\ Income\ Associated\ with\ Moving\ Up\ 2\ Selectivity\ Levels}{Increase\ in\ Tuition\ Cost\ Associated\ with\ Moving\ Up\ 2\ Selectivity\ Levels}$$

Based on Student Paying "List Price" for Private Colleges and In-State Tuition for Public Colleges

	Private College to Private College Move			Public College to Private College Move		
	Men Who Entered College in:			Men Who Entered College in:		
	1960	1972	1982	1960	1972	1982
from Rank 3 to Rank 1 College	32.7	101.5	189.6	13.8	16.4	21.4
from Rank 4 to Rank 2 College	44.0	51.3	61.1	21.6	10.5	16.5
from Rank 5 to Rank 3 College	39.8	16.1	21.0	29.9	11.1	19.4
from Rank 6 to Rank 4 College	83.1	7.6	48.0	49.6	8.7	20.9
from Rank 7 to Rank 5 College	129.0	21.8	69.6	55.4	12.1	27.1
from Rank 8 to Rank 6 College	200.7	56.6	41.3	63.5	20.1	19.0

Based on Student Paying Average Tuition Paid (both in Private and Public Colleges)

	Private College to Private College Move			Public College to Private College Move		
	Men Who Entered College in:			Men Who Entered College in:		
	1960	1972	1982	1960	1972	1982
from Rank 3 to Rank 1 College	na	103.8	182.5	na	17.0	24.1
from Rank 4 to Rank 2 College	na	13.0	35.8	na	11.5	19.5
from Rank 5 to Rank 3 College	na	23.9	25.8	na	13.7	22.0
from Rank 6 to Rank 4 College	na	8.1	40.1	na	10.6	22.5
from Rank 7 to Rank 5 College	na	27.6	56.0	na	14.6	28.6
from Rank 8 to Rank 6 College	na	81.7	48.6	na	24.8	22.1

Estimates are based on a working life of thirty-four years and a 0 percent discount rate. Career income estimates are based on the age-earnings profile in the 1995 *Current Population Survey*. Career income estimates for top-ranked colleges are underestimated owing to topcoding (censoring of high incomes) and the estimation method used (see Appendix A). The abbreviation *na* indicates that measures of tuition paid are not available for 1960. Approximate estimates for a 3 percent discount rate may be computed by multiplying the numbers in the table by 0.5.

Some of the ratios shown in Table 2.5 are very large. For instance, among men who entered private colleges in 1982, the ratio of earnings difference to the cost difference between rank 1 and rank 3 colleges is 189.6. This ratio is large not only because there are significant career income differences between the men but also because there are very small tuition differences between the colleges. Table 2.5 shows that the ratios of income differences to cost differences have been growing over time for students in highly selective colleges. For instance, the statistic cited above is 32.7 for 1960 entrants, 101.5 for 1972 entrants, and 189.6 for 1982 entrants.

Table 2.6 presents the statistics in Table 2.5 in a more accessible way. It shows the number of years that a graduate from a more selective college needs to earn before he "breaks even"—that is, covers his increased tuition costs. The smallest numbers in Table 2.6 are less than 1 (only a few months of higher earnings are necessary to break even), and the largest numbers are around 4 (four years of higher earnings are necessary to break even). Because public college tuition is subsidized by tax dollars, the number of years needed to break even on a public-to-private college move is naturally larger than the number needed to break even on a similar private-to-private college move. I will not dwell on the statistics in Tables 2.5 and 2.6 because they are not corrected for aptitude. It would be unwise, for instance, to interpret them in a causal way or as a return on investment.

The Return to Investing in a More Selective College

Tables 2.7 through 2.9 repeat the exercise of Tables 2.4 through 2.6, except that earnings have been corrected for differences in measured college aptitude. I regressed individuals' earnings at age thirty-two on their college admissions test scores, standardized test scores in English and mathematics, and high school grade point averages. I then predicted what each individual would earn if he had average measured aptitude and computed earnings by college rank group using the predicted earnings rather than actual earnings. Appendix B describes this procedure in more detail. The correction can be carried out for men who entered college in 1972 and 1982 because the two recent longitudinal surveys include the measures of individual aptitude listed above. The correction cannot be carried out for men who entered college in 1960 because the *Occupational Changes in a Generation* survey lacks similar measures.

Table 2.7 shows that controlling for aptitude eliminates the majority (between two-thirds and three-quarters), but not all, of the income differences between college rank groups. That is, if we compare two men with the same measured aptitude, the one who graduates from a more selective college still tends to earn more over his career. Among 1982 private college entrants, the career income

TABLE 2.6.   YEARS OF EARNINGS NEEDED TO BREAK EVEN ON COST OF MOVING UP TWO SELECTIVITY LEVELS

Not Corrected for College Aptitude

Based on Student Paying "List Price" for Private Colleges and In-State Tuition for Public Colleges

	Private College to Private College Move			Public College to Private College Move		
	Men Who Entered College in:			Men Who Entered College in:		
	1960	1972	1982	1960	1972	1982
from Rank 3 to Rank 1 College	1.0	0.3	0.2	2.5	2.1	1.6
from Rank 4 to Rank 2 College	0.8	0.7	0.6	1.6	3.2	2.1
from Rank 5 to Rank 3 College	0.9	2.1	1.6	1.1	3.1	1.8
from Rank 6 to Rank 4 College	0.4	4.5	0.7	0.7	3.9	1.6
from Rank 7 to Rank 5 College	0.3	1.6	0.5	0.6	2.8	1.3
from Rank 8 to Rank 6 College	0.2	0.6	0.8	0.5	1.7	1.8

Based on Student Paying Average Tuition Paid (both in Private and Public Colleges)

	Private College to Private College Move			Public College to Private College Move		
	Men Who Entered College in:			Men Who Entered College in:		
	1960	1972	1982	1960	1972	1982
from Rank 3 to Rank 1 College	na	0.1	0.2	na	0.9	1.4
from Rank 4 to Rank 2 College	na	2.6	1.0	na	3.0	1.7
from Rank 5 to Rank 3 College	na	1.4	1.3	na	2.5	1.5
from Rank 6 to Rank 4 College	na	4.2	0.8	na	3.2	1.5
from Rank 7 to Rank 5 College	na	1.2	0.6	na	2.3	1.2
from Rank 8 to Rank 6 College	na	0.4	0.7	na	1.4	1.5

Estimates are based on a working life of thirty-four years and a 0 percent discount rate. Career income estimates are based on the age-earnings profile in the 1995 *Current Population Survey.* Career income estimates for top-ranked colleges are underestimated owing to topcoding (censoring of high incomes) and the estimation method used (see Appendix A). The abbreviation *na* indicates that measures of tuition paid are not available for 1960. Approximate estimates for a 3 percent discount rate may be computed by multiplying the numbers in the table by 2.

TABLE 2.7. CAREER INCOME BY COLLEGE SELECTIVITY, 1997 DOLLARS

	Corrected for College Aptitude			
	Men Who Entered College in 1972:		*Men Who Entered College in 1982:*	
	Private Colleges	Public Colleges	Private Colleges	Public Colleges
Rank 1 Colleges	$2,240,995	nc	$2,462,036	nc
Rank 2 Colleges	$2,096,134	$2,019,608	$2,360,878	$2,138,587
Rank 3 Colleges	$2,017,529	$1,970,466	$2,190,843	$2,067,522
Rank 4 Colleges	$2,004,449	$1,957,691	$2,166,801	$1,968,297
Rank 5 Colleges	$1,972,728	$1,950,540	$2,148,551	$1,921,379
Rank 6 Colleges	$1,971,566	$1,925,846	$2,068,946	$1,918,786
Rank 7 Colleges	$1,918,695	$1,878,721	$1,992,543	$1,824,592
Rank 8 Colleges	$1,878,721	$1,809,957	$1,986,344	$1,815,392

Estimates are based on a working life of thirty-four years and a 0 percent discount rate. Career income estimates are based on the age-earnings profile in the 1995 *Current Population Survey.* Career income estimates for top-ranked colleges are underestimated owing to topcoding (censoring of high incomes) and the estimation method used (see Appendix A). The correction for measured college aptitude is based on coefficients from a regression of individuals' earnings on their college admissions test scores, other standardized test scores, and high school grade point averages (see Appendix B). The abbreviation *nc* indicates that there are no public colleges in the rank 1 group. 1960 estimates are not available because the *Occupational Changes in a Generation* survey does not include individual aptitude measures. Approximate estimates for a 3 percent discount rate may be computed by multiplying the numbers in the table by 0.5. The price deflator used for putting dollars of the day into 1997 dollars is the consumer durable goods price index.

difference between rank 1 and rank 3 graduates with the same measured aptitude is about $100,000. The difference between rank 2 and rank 4 graduates with the same measured aptitude is about $200,000. Most career income differences by college rank are growing over time.

Table 2.8 presents the ratios of return to investment for a student who hypothetically moves up two selectivity levels. Since the returns have been corrected by aptitude measures that are used for college admissions, it is reasonable to think of a student choosing between colleges to which he has already been admitted and that are located two ranks apart. That is, the correction for aptitude probably does a reasonably good job of eliminating the effects of selection by colleges. (Self-selection on the part of students is a more open issue and one to which I will return.) Like Table 2.5, Table 2.8 shows estimates for full tuition and average tuition paid and analyzes private-to-private college moves as well as public-to-private college moves.

TABLE 2.8. RATIO OF RETURN TO INVESTMENT FOR MOVING UP TWO SELECTIVITY LEVELS

Corrected for College Aptitude

$$Ratio\ of\ Return\ to\ Investment = \frac{Increase\ in\ Career\ Income\ for\ Moving\ Up\ 2\ Selectivity\ Levels}{Increase\ in\ Tuition\ Payments\ for\ Moving\ Up\ 2\ Selectivity\ Levels}$$

Based on Student Paying "List Price" for Private Colleges and In-State Tuition for Public Colleges

	Private College to Private College Move		Public College to Private College Move	
	Men Who Entered College in:		Men Who Entered College in:	
	1972	1982	1972	1982
from Rank 3 to Rank 1 College	104.1	128.5	11.1	13.7
from Rank 4 to Rank 2 College	51.8	63.0	6.1	14.7
from Rank 5 to Rank 3 College	12.6	7.2	3.2	10.4
from Rank 6 to Rank 4 College	5.8	14.6	3.6	9.8
from Rank 7 to Rank 5 College	10.2	25.5	4.9	15.3
from Rank 8 to Rank 6 College	12.9	10.0	9.2	12.6

Based on Student Paying Average Tuition Paid (both in Private and Public Colleges)

	Private College to Private College Move		Public College to Private College Move	
	Men Who Entered College in:		Men Who Entered College in:	
	1972	1982	1972	1982
from Rank 3 to Rank 1 College	120.2	123.7	14.8	15.4
from Rank 4 to Rank 2 College	21.5	36.9	6.7	17.3
from Rank 5 to Rank 3 College	18.7	8.8	3.9	11.8
from Rank 6 to Rank 4 College	6.2	12.2	4.3	10.6
from Rank 7 to Rank 5 College	12.9	20.5	5.9	16.2
from Rank 8 to Rank 6 College	18.7	11.8	11.3	14.6

Estimates are based on a working life of thirty-four years and a 0 percent discount rate. Career income estimates are based on the age-earnings profile in the 1995 *Current Population Survey.* Career income estimates for top-ranked colleges are underestimated owing to topcoding (censoring of high incomes) and the estimation method used (see Appendix A). The correction for measured college aptitude is based on coefficients from a regression of individuals' earnings on their college admissions test scores, other standardized test scores, and high school grade point averages (see Appendix B). 1960 estimates are not available because the *Occupational Changes in a Generation* survey does not include individual aptitude measures. Approximate estimates for a 3 percent discount rate may be computed by multiplying the numbers in the table by 0.5.

The ratios of return to investment vary widely, depending on which ranks the student is moving to and from and whether the lower ranked college is public or private. The ratios are growing over time, indicating that attending a more selective college is an increasingly attractive investment. The best investments tend to be moves among highly selective colleges (from rank 3 to rank 1, from rank 4 to rank 2), but moving away from the minimally selective group of colleges (from rank 8 to rank 6) also tends to be a good investment. The very large ratios for moving between rank 3 and rank 1 private colleges (or rank 4 and rank 2 private colleges) are generated not only by the career income differences shown in the previous table but also by the very small tuition differences between the colleges.

Table 2.9 presents the statistics in Table 2.8 in their more accessible form: the number of years it takes a student to break even on his investment in a more selective college. For private-to-private college moves, the number of years needed to break even ranges from 0.3 (rank 3 to rank 1 moves) to 5.8 (rank 6 to rank 4 moves). For public-to-private college moves, the number of years ranges from about 2 (rank 3 to rank 1; rank 4 to rank 2) to 10.6 (rank 5 to rank 3). Most students would earn back their investment in a few years; in no case would a student have to work more than a third of a normal working life to earn back his investment.

The career incomes corrected for aptitude can be used for a number of additional thought experiments. They can even be used to form predictions of the return to investment for current (1997) college freshmen, although the accuracy of such predictions will naturally be contingent on the United States earnings distribution remaining as it is. In Tables 2.10 and 2.11, I offer a few interesting thought experiments and predictions, with the caveat that I have made no attempt to forecast future earnings distributions.

Table 2.10 shows comprehensive college costs, by rank group, for 1972, 1982, and 1997 (all in 1997 dollars). One must be wary about comparing comprehensive costs across colleges because differences in the typical "package" offered affects reported costs. For instance, board plans tend to be minimal at colleges that have a majority of their students living in off-campus housing. The information in Table 2.10 is needed, however, for the thought experiments in Table 2.11.

Table 2.11 shows what 1997 freshmen might anticipate gaining by moving up two selectivity levels. Although I must assume that they will have career incomes like those of 1982 college entrants, I use actual 1997–1998 tuition. That is, the students are assumed to pay 1997–1998 *real* tuition for four years (tuition will rise at the same pace as inflation). The top panel of Table 2.11 shows ratios of returns to investment; the bottom panel shows years needed to break even.

The first thing to observe in Table 2.11 is the curious fact that rank 3 private colleges tend to charge higher tuition (full tuition and average tuition paid) than rank 1 private colleges, so that a student who moves from a private rank 3

TABLE 2.9. YEARS OF EARNINGS NEEDED TO BREAK EVEN ON MOVING UP TWO SELECTIVITY LEVELS

Corrected for College Aptitude

Based on Student Paying "List Price" for Private Colleges and In-State Tuition for Public Colleges

	Private College to Private College Move		Public College to Private College Move	
	Men Who Entered College in:		Men Who Entered College in:	
	1972	1982	1972	1982
from Rank 3 to Rank 1 College	0.3	0.3	3.1	2.5
from Rank 4 to Rank 2 College	0.7	0.5	5.5	2.3
from Rank 5 to Rank 3 College	2.7	4.7	10.6	3.3
from Rank 6 to Rank 4 College	5.8	2.3	9.6	3.5
from Rank 7 to Rank 5 College	3.3	1.3	6.9	2.2
from Rank 8 to Rank 6 College	2.6	3.4	3.7	2.7

Based on Student Paying Average Tuition Paid (both in Private and Public Colleges)

	Private College to Private College Move		Public College to Private College Move	
	Men Who Entered College in:		Men Who Entered College in:	
	1972	1982	1972	1982
from Rank 3 to Rank 1 College	0.3	0.3	2.1	2.1
from Rank 4 to Rank 2 College	1.6	0.9	5.1	2.0
from Rank 5 to Rank 3 College	1.8	3.8	8.6	2.9
from Rank 6 to Rank 4 College	5.5	2.8	7.9	3.2
from Rank 7 to Rank 5 College	2.6	1.7	5.8	2.1
from Rank 8 to Rank 6 College	1.8	2.9	3.0	2.3

Estimates are based on a working life of thirty-four years and a 0 percent discount rate. Career income estimates are based on the age-earnings profile in the 1995 *Current Population Survey*. Career income estimates for top-ranked colleges are underestimated owing to topcoding (censoring of high incomes) and the estimation method used (see Appendix A). The correction for measured college aptitude is based on coefficients from a regression of individuals' earnings on their college admissions test scores, other standardized test scores, and high school grade point averages (see Appendix B). 1960 estimates are not available because the *Occupational Changes in a Generation* survey does not include individual aptitude measures. Approximate estimates for a 3 percent discount rate may be computed by multiplying the numbers in the table by 2.

TABLE 2.10.   COMPREHENSIVE COLLEGE COSTS (TUITION, FEES, ROOM, AND BOARD) IN 1997 DOLLARS

Comprehensive costs are not strictly comparable between colleges that have different residence patterns (on- vs. off-campus, dormitory vs. fraternity/sorority housing).

	Private Colleges			Public Colleges		
	1972	1982	1997	1972	1982	1997
Rank 1 Colleges	$10,116	$11,512	$27,596	nc	nc	nc
Rank 2 Colleges	$10,986	$12,053	$27,218	$2,942	$3,315	$10,834
Rank 3 Colleges	$10,084	$10,761	$26,388	$2,722	$2,971	$ 8,873
Rank 4 Colleges	$ 9,789	$10,724	$25,475	$5,000	$4,855	$10,505
Rank 5 Colleges	$ 9,075	$ 9,444	$23,693	$4,176	$3,911	$ 9,000
Rank 6 Colleges	$ 7,717	$ 8,239	$20,568	$3,095	$3,100	$ 8,230
Rank 7 Colleges	$ 7,158	$ 7,306	$18,055	$3,422	$3,209	$ 7,753
Rank 8 Colleges	$ 5,859	$ 5,912	$13,933	$3,038	$2,794	$ 6,015

Colleges report "typical" room and board charges, which vary with housing patterns, the usual number of meals taken, and so on. Measures of comprehensive cost are not available for 1960. The abbreviation *nc* indicates that there are no public colleges in the rank 1 group. The price deflator used for putting dollars of the day into 1997 dollars is the consumer durable goods price index.

college to a private rank 1 college makes no financial investment at all. Of course, the student might be offered more merit aid at the lower ranked college. To explore this possibility, some of the statistics in Table 2.11 represent an extreme form of merit aid—a "free ride" at the lower ranked college versus paying full comprehensive costs at the higher ranked college. If a student has a free ride, his college covers his comprehensive costs (tuition, fees, room, and board).

The ratios of returns to investment for moving up two selectivity levels are lower for 1997 entrants than for 1982 entrants. (This is because real tuition is higher; career incomes are identical by assumption.) All of the investments are still, however, attractive. For instance, a person moving from a rank 5 private college to a rank 3 private college can expect to earn his investment back three times over during his career. This is one of the lower ratios shown in the table: moves from rank 4 to rank 2 and from rank 3 to rank 1 are much more attractive investments. The predictions that use average tuition paid or comprehensive costs are broadly similar to those that use full tuition.

The column at the far right of each of the subpanels in Table 2.11 shows the results of the free ride experiment. This represents an extreme choice, rather than a choice that many students are realistically given the opportunity to consider.

TABLE 2.11. PREDICTIONS FOR 1997 COLLEGE ENTRANTS

Predictions use actual 1997–98 tuition and assume that 1997 college entrants have the same earnings patterns as 1982 college entrants (the most recent students who have income histories long enough to permit estimation of career income).

Ratio of Return to Investment for Moving Up Two Selectivity Levels
Corrected for College Aptitude

	Private College to Private College Move				Public College to Private College Move			
	full tuition to full tuition	average tuition paid to average tuition paid	compre-hensive cost to compre-hensive cost	free ride to compre-hensive cost	full tuition to full tuition	average tuition paid to average tuition paid	compre-hensive cost to compre-hensive cost	free ride to compre-hensive cost
from Rank 3 to Rank 1	not defined (rank 3 costs more than rank 1)		56.1	3.4	6.3	30.1	5.3	5.0
from Rank 4 to Rank 2	67.4	17.5	27.8	2.3	5.9	17.2	5.9	4.7
from Rank 5 to Rank 3	3.0	2.8	3.9	0.5	4.0	10.2	3.9	3.2
from Rank 6 to Rank 4	5.0	5.8	5.0	1.2	3.7	9.6	3.6	3.1
from Rank 7 to Rank 5	8.0	8.1	6.9	2.2	5.7	15.3	5.1	4.6
from Rank 8 to Rank 6	3.5	4.1	3.1	1.4	4.9	12.2	4.4	4.2

Years of Earnings Needed to Break Even on Moving Up Two Selectivity Levels
Corrected for College Aptitude

	Private College to Private College Move				Public College to Private College Move			
	full tuition to full tuition	average tuition paid to average tuition paid	compre-hensive cost to compre-hensive cost	free ride to compre-hensive cost	full tuition to full tuition	average tuition paid to average tuition paid	compre-hensive cost to compre-hensive cost	free ride to compre-hensive cost
from Rank 3 to Rank 1	0	0	0.6	10.0	5.4	1.1	6.5	6.9
from Rank 4 to Rank 2	0.5	1.9	1.2	14.6	5.8	2.0	5.8	7.2
from Rank 5 to Rank 3	11.4	11.9	8.7	67.7	8.6	3.3	8.8	10.6
from Rank 6 to Rank 4	6.8	5.9	6.8	28.0	9.1	3.6	9.5	11.0
from Rank 7 to Rank 5	4.3	4.2	4.9	15.3	6.0	2.2	6.7	7.4
from Rank 8 to Rank 6	9.6	8.2	10.9	25.1	6.9	2.8	7.8	8.2

While offers of free rides are not rare *events*, they are rare events for moves of only two selectivity levels. For instance, most students who are admitted to rank 1 colleges receive free ride offers only from colleges in rank 4 or below (if they receive such offers at all). The surprise of Table 2.11 is not that *some* offers of free rides are better monetary deals than the alternative of paying full comprehensive costs at a college ranked 2 groups higher. We expect this. Rather the surprise is that many offers of free rides do not appear to be better deals, and a number of offers are not even "close calls." For instance, the numbers suggest that a student should take the free ride if he has a free ride at a rank 5 private college but would have to pay comprehensive costs at a rank 3 private college. In contrast, the numbers suggest that a student should reject the free ride if he has a free ride at rank 3 private college but would have to pay comprehensive costs at a rank 1 private college; he is predicted to earn his investment back 3.4 times over during his career. It is worth noting that free rides from public colleges are not nearly as attractive as free rides from similarly ranked private colleges. This is because public college tuition is already subsidized by tax dollars so that the free ride is not a very big discount.

Comments on Controlling for Aptitude and Some Caveats

It is impossible to know when one has controlled sufficiently for aptitude, so we might worry that the results shown above are too favorable toward more selective colleges because they benefit from their students' unobserved ability—that is, ability that is only weakly correlated with admissions test scores, other standardized test scores, and grades. On the other hand, the estimation methods (especially top-coding and career income estimates based on the *Current Population Survey*) are unfavorable to more selective colleges because their graduates' incomes are systemically understated. We cannot know exactly where the balance lies between these offsetting biases. However, it is possible to say something more about the adequacy of the controls for aptitude.

The measures I use to control for aptitude are important factors in most colleges' admission processes. This suggests that the correction for aptitude probably does a good job of eliminating the effects of selection on the part of colleges. That is, the moves analyzed in Tables 2.8, 2.9, and 2.11 are realistic in the sense that we are examining students who probably do have both options open to them (they would be admitted by the higher ranked college). The correction for aptitude does less to eliminate the effects of self-selection on the part of students. That is, some students may refuse admission offers from more selective colleges because they know something about their own abilities or earnings capacity that colleges could not know. For instance, a student might know that he would not thrive in a competitive atmosphere. Or a student might know that he wants to pursue a career, such as the ministry, that offers unusually low earnings for someone of his ability. (I found no evidence in the data, however, that people who went to low-ranked colleges for someone of their ability were more likely to pursue careers in public service. If anything, the data show the opposite pattern.) In any case, some of the apparent returns to graduating from a more selective college may actually be attributable to the self-selection of students who have low earnings potential into less competitive colleges.

In the interests of brevity, I have not shown estimates that I computed for completeness but that would not have altered the overall pattern of results. For instance, career income estimates based on the *Panel Survey of Income* dynamics are similar to the estimates shown, except that they contain higher earnings growth for graduates from highly selective colleges. Using them increases the income differences by college rank. I have not shown results for different discount rates, but I have indicated the effect of a 3 percent real discount rate in the note that accompanies each table.

Summary

The calculations in this chapter indicate that people who invest in education at a more selective college generally earn back their investment several times over during their careers. This statement holds across the entire spectrum of colleges, although moving to a more selective college is generally a better investment for students who have the aptitude to attend a rank 1, rank 2, or rank 3 college. In many cases, even students who are offered a "free ride" by a lower ranked college would maximize their monetary worth by refusing the aid and attending the higher ranked college. Since 1972, the returns to attending a more selective college have been rising over time. For students with the aptitude to attend a rank 1 or rank 2 college, the returns to attending a more selective college have been rising over the *entire* period since 1960.

Appendix A: Estimating Career Earnings Using Empirical-Age Earnings Profiles

I used two methods to estimate career earnings from earnings at age thirty-two. The first is the preferred method for cross section data, and the second is the preferred method for longitudinal data.

There are three advantages to using cross section data: the age-earnings profile is up-to-date, the number of survey respondents is large, and the researcher does not have to account for inflation. The disadvantage of using cross section data is that, while each individual sets his own earnings *level*, all individuals must share the same pattern of earnings *growth*. We know that people who graduate from more selective colleges tend to have higher earnings growth as well as higher earnings levels; so using cross section data generates career earnings that are underestimates for graduates of highly selective colleges.

The advantage of using longitudinal data (a survey that follows the same individuals over their lifetimes) is that one can model individual earnings growth as well as individual earnings levels. There are three disadvantages of using longitudinal data: a mixture of past and present age-earnings profiles are simultaneously used so that time trends in the profiles are suppressed, the number of survey respondents is small (relative to cross section data), and the quality of the age-earnings profile depends on the quality of the adjustment for inflation. Because this method suppresses time trends, it generates career earnings that are underestimates for graduates of highly selective colleges during periods when income inequality is rising, like the current period.

Thus both methods understate the career incomes of graduates of more selective colleges relative to graduates of less selective colleges. This underestimation cannot be avoided without making restrictive assumptions. It is probably best to accept the fact that career incomes for highly selective colleges are *conservatively estimated*.

Murphy and Welch (1990) demonstrate that quartic equations for log earnings capture most of the information in age-earnings data, so I adopt quartic specifications.

The Method for Cross Section Data

The *Current Population Survey* is the 1-in-1000 rotating sample of the United States population that is used for computing most common labor force statistics, such as the unemployment rate. I estimated the following quartic equation for males who held baccalaureate degrees and worked full-time in 1995.

$$\ln(Earnings_i) = \alpha_0 + \alpha_1 Age_i + \alpha_2 Age_i^2 + \alpha_3 Age_i^3 + \alpha_4 Age_i^4 + \varepsilon_i$$

The coefficients from this equation are used to predict career earnings for each individual for whom I have earnings at age thirty-two in one of the three following surveys: *Occupational Changes in a Generation*, the *National Longitudinal Study of the Class of 1972*, and the *National Longitudinal Survey of Youth*. Each individual sets his own earnings level—that is, the prediction incorporates an individual-specific intercept.

The Method for Longitudinal Data

The *Panel Survey of Income Dynamics* is the largest long-panel survey of the United States population. It covers the period from 1968 to the present. I estimated the following equation for males who held baccalaureate degrees, worked full-time, and were between age forty and age sixty-five in 1995. The equation allows both the level and growth rate of earnings to be quartic in age.

$$\ln(Earnings_i) = Earn32_i + \beta_1 Age_i + \beta_2 Age_i^2 + \beta_3 Age_i^3 + \beta_4 Age_i^4 +$$
$$Earn32_i \cdot Age_i + Earn32_i \cdot Age_i^2 + Earn32_i \cdot Age_i^3 +$$
$$Earn32_i \cdot Age_i^4 + \varepsilon_i$$

The coefficients from this equation are used to predict career earnings for individuals in the three surveys named above. The predicted level and growth of earnings are specific to each individual.

Appendix B: Correcting for Measured College Aptitude

To correct for college aptitude, I estimated the following regression:

$$\ln(Earn32_i) = \gamma_0 + \gamma_1 SATMath_i + \gamma_2 SATVerbal_i + \gamma_3 StdEnglish_i +$$
$$\gamma_4 StdMath_i + \gamma_5 GPA + \xi_i$$

separately for the *National Longitudinal Study of the Class of 1972* and the *National Longitudinal Survey of Youth*. I used the estimated coefficients from this regression to predict the earnings each individual would have if he had average aptitude (among people in the relevant survey). That is, I calculated:

$$\ln(Earn32_i) - \hat{\gamma}_1 SATMath_i - \hat{\gamma}_2 SATVerbal_i - \hat{\gamma}_3 StdEnglish_i - \hat{\gamma}_4 StdMath_i -$$
$$\overline{\gamma_5 GPA_i + \hat{\gamma}_1 SATMath + \hat{\gamma}_2 SATVerbal + \hat{\gamma}_3 StdEnglish + \hat{\gamma}_4 StdMath_i + \hat{\gamma}_5 GPA}$$

These predicted earnings are used to compute the career income, adjusted for aptitude, shown in Table 2.7.

One could also adjust for demographic, such as race, parents' education, and family income. Such adjustments make the return to attending a more selective college increase more over time. The reason is that highly selective colleges have increasingly admitted students who come from backgrounds that are generally not propitious for earnings.

Endnotes

1. See Blackburn and Neumark (1993); Cawley, Heckman, and Vytlacil (1998); Freeman and Katz (1994); Heckman (1995); Heckman, Cawley, Conneely, and Vytlacil (1996); Juhn,

Murphy, and Pierce (1993); Katz and Murphy (1992); Levy, Murnane, and Willett (1995); and Murnane, Willett, Duhaldeborde, and Tyler (1998).

2. Kane (1995) is a good starting place in this literature.

3. More generally, the choice among colleges generates differences in most components of the opportunity cost that are trivial in comparison to differences in tuition and earnings.

4. The superscripts A and B indicate the colleges. Years are indexed by the subscript t, and counting effectively begins at the beginning of the freshman academic year. The subscript i indexes individual students, because tuition, fees, and grants can vary across individuals, depending on their undergraduate program, state of residence, need, merit, and so on.

5. These sums assume that a person has a working life of thirty-four years. Empirical age-earnings profiles are used for the calculations that follow, and these naturally take account of the low working hours in a person's twenties and sixties. See previous note for the definitions of the superscripts and subscripts.

6. That is, the people who entered college in 1982 are typically age thirty-two in 1994 or 1995. If I were to use earnings at age forty, say, the most recent college entrants whom I could examine would have been freshmen in 1974. For an empirical exercise of this kind, it would be a poor idea to use earnings at an age less than thirty because so many individuals with high aptitude have irregular earnings in their twenties, owing to their taking internships, attending graduate and professional school, and so on. The *National Longitudinal Study of the Class of 1972* and the *National Longitudinal Survey of Youth* report several years of earnings for each individual, but *Occupational Changes in a Generation* reports earnings only in 1972.

7. Also, the dispersion of SAT scores has increased over time. The change in dispersion is, however, of little empirical significance compared to the change in the mean SAT score.

8. Each college's reported average SAT scores are converted into percentile scores, and an enrollment-weighted average percentile score is computed for each rank group. It would be preferable (and different) to convert each individual student's SAT scores into percentile scores and then take the average within each rank group. The latter statistic cannot be computed, unfortunately.

9. Nonselective colleges typically do not report average admissions test scores. However, their draw from the aptitude distribution may be inferred by eliminating the students who attend colleges that fit into one of the eight rank groups.

10. The tendency to sort not only affects differences between rank groups (as shown in the table), but differences between colleges within a rank group. In Hoxby (1997b), I show that the dispersion in SAT scores within each college has fallen over time.

11. Some of the United States military academies may belong in rank group 1, but, like other specialized colleges, they are omitted from the analysis.

12. A good price deflator for incomes also tends to be a good cost deflator for colleges, since salaries form so large a share of their costs. I use the consumer durable goods price index as a deflator because it places less weight than the CPI does on gasoline and other consumer goods that have had significant, *real* price changes between 1960 and the present.

13. Colorado School of Mines, University of California–Berkeley, College of William and Mary, Georgia Institute of Technology, and University of Virginia.

14. See Hoxby (1997b) for an analysis of the tuition rise that focuses on the increasing competitiveness of the market for college education. See Clotfelter (1996) for a contrasting analysis that emphasizes rising demand for education combined with colleges' having market power that allows them to let costs grow without discipline during periods of rising demand.

15. For instance, the topcode for 1995 income of thirty-two-year-olds is $150,000, so that high earners have "$150,000 or more" reported. In practice, topcoding makes analyses of the mean and median income for the top-rank groups very similar. If there were no topcoding, it would be appropriate to analyze median incomes for the top-ranked groups in order to predict returns for a typical student. It would be appropriate to analyze mean incomes in order to predict other variables, such as future contributions to the endowment.

16. This rule of thumb is based in actual computations for a 3 percent discount rate.

References

Barron's Educational Series. *Barron's Profiles of American Colleges.* Various editions. Hauppauge, N.Y.: Barron's Educational Series, 1980.

Blackburn, M. L. and Neumark, D. "Omitted Ability Bias and the Increase in the Return to Schooling." *Journal of Labor Economics,* 1993, *11*(3).

Blau, P. M., Duncan, O. D., Featherman, D. L., and Hauser, R. M. *Occupational Changes in a Generation, 1962 and 1973* [computer file]. Madison: University of Wisconsin [producer], 1983. Ann Arbor: Inter-university Consortium for Political and Social Research [distributor], 1994.

Cawley, J., Heckman, J., and Vytlacil, E. "Cognitive Ability and the Rising Return to Education." NBER Working Paper No. 6388, 1998.

Center for Human Resource Research. *National Longitudinal Survey of the Class of 1972, Fifth Follow-Up.* Columbus: Center for Human Resource Research, The Ohio State University, 1986.

Center for Human Resource Research. *National Longitudinal Survey of Youth.* Columbus: Center for Human Resource Research, The Ohio State University, 1997.

Clotfelter, C. T. *Buying the Best: Cost Escalation in Elite Higher Education.* NBER Monograph. Princeton, N.J.: Princeton University Press, 1996.

Freeman, R. and Katz, L. "Rising Wage Inequality: The U.S. vs. Other Advanced Countries." In R. Freeman (ed.), *Working Under Different Rules.* New York: Russell Sage Foundation, 1994.

Heckman, J. "Lessons from the Bell Curve." *Journal of Political Economy,* 1995, *103*(5), 1091–1120.

Heckman, J., Cawley, J., Conneely, K., and Vytlacil, E. "Measuring the Effects of Cognitive Ability." National Bureau of Economic Research Working Paper No. 5645, 1996.

Hoxby, C. "The Changing Market Structure of U.S. Higher Education: 1940–1990." Mimeo, Harvard University Department of Economics, 1997a.

Hoxby, C. "How the Changing Market Structure of American College Education Explains Tuition." National Bureau of Economic Research Working Paper No. 6323, 1997b.

Hoxby, C. and Terry, B. "Explaining Rising Wage and Income Inequality among the College-Educated." National Bureau of Economic Research Working Paper, 1998.

Juhn, C., Murphy, K., and Pierce, B. "Wage Inequality and the Rise in Returns to Skills." *Journal of Political Economy,* 1993, *101*(3), 410–442.

Kane, T. "Rising Public College Tuition and College Entry." National Bureau of Economic Research Working Paper No. 4124, 1995.

Katz, L. and Murphy, K. "Changes in Relative Wages, 1963–1987: Supply and Demand Factors." *Quarterly Journal of Economics,* 1992, *107*(1), 35–78.

Levy, F., Murnane, R. J., and Willett, J. B. "The Growing Importance of Cognitive Skills in Wage Determination." *Review of Economics and Statistics,* 1995, 77(2), 251–266.

Murnane, R. J., Willett, J. B., Duhaldeborde, Y., and Tyler, J. H. "The Role of Cognitive Skills in Explaining Recent Trends in the U.S. Distribution of Earned Income." Mimeo, Harvard Graduate School of Education, 1998.

Murphy, K. and Welch, F. "Empirical Age-Earnings Profiles," *Journal of Labor Economics,* 1990, *8*(2), 202–229.

CHAPTER THREE

THE IDEA OF ORGANIC GROWTH IN HIGHER EDUCATION

James Engell

Engell attributes the decline of the humanities in higher education to three factors, all of which are related to money. He stresses the need for today's campus leaders to reexamine and establish the essential purposes and functions of higher learning and outlines a model centered on the entelechy of higher education. This entelechy—the coordinated fulfillment of several different goals and goods—can serve as a guide for educational leaders, helping them to take decisive action that will shape organic, institutional growth rather than reacting to imposed, external forces largely beyond their control.

It is clear that higher education may not be afforded the opportunity to undergo organic change, stemming from within at its own pace, but rather will likely be subject to external forces and threats that compel swift and systemic change in the nation's traditional colleges and universities.

DEVLIN **(1999)**

New inventions, fresh discoveries, alterations in the markets of the world throw accustomed methods and the men who are accustomed to them out of date and use without pause or pity.

WILSON **(1909)**

We employ various models—economic, historical, or managerial—to address the accelerating changes that now are sweeping higher education. Without relying on any particular discipline in the humanities, this chapter offers a broadly humanistic model. The first step in creating such a model is to ascertain the purposes and functions, the *entelechy,* of higher education. *Entelechy* means the striving for perfection in a series of goals taken together as a whole. The word comes from the Greek *enteles*, meaning complete or full, which in turn derives from *telos*, or goal. An entelechy demands we envision how to fulfill the potential of the whole by co-ordinating and giving proper relative weight to a set of varied goals and the goods they seek to achieve. For each institution, this entails a particular inflection or emphasis. "The single most serious problem of our universities is their failure to adhere steadily to their own purposes," states Hanna Gray. "No university is strong," Bart Giamatti claims, "if it is unsure of its purpose and nature" (Axtell, 1998, pp. 213–214).

The entelechy of higher education involves an instrumental economic good, an associative intellectual and social good, an instrumental civic and political good, and two final goods: one moral or ethical and the other the seeking of knowledge and ideas for their own sake, which is the final cause of all the other goods.

Education acts inevitably as an instrumental good; it readies individuals to undertake specific tasks, careers, and professions. To insist on knowledge as a good in itself while refusing to consider its application is impractical except in repressive regimes. It conjures up a caricature of the ivory tower, akin to Laputa in Swift's *Gulliver's Travels,* where inhabitants, knowing only abstract math and music, cannot use a plumb line to build houses, which collapse randomly and kill citizens. Basic skills support any economic undertaking; much education as an instrumental good must occur by the time mandatory schooling ceases, one reason Hedrick Smith extols German and Japanese secondary systems (Smith, 1995, p. 100–125). If we are sensible enough to get our children to a genuine twelfth-grade level of literacy and numeracy (admittedly, a large "if"), this instrumental good will be well on its way. But in a technological, complex society, higher education and professional schools continue this instrumental function, which, as an economic good, is assumed, supported, and promoted by an increasing number of colleges and universities in practice, marketing, and mission statements. Public universities, such as the system in Massachusetts, advertise the personal economic returns to higher education on radio as their chief asset for applicants to consider. The word *success*—meaning individual economic success—punctuates college advertisements and redrafted mottoes. Politicians press hard for it. Parents demand it. Life insurance companies remind clients of it. Businesses often see it as the raison d'être of education.

Beginning in the early 1980s, money came to be seen, for many Americans, as a good in itself, an end rather than a means, something automatically conferring status, class, power, even virtue (Lapham, 1988; Taylor, 1989, pp. 1–21). Moreover, in terms of economic changes and behaviors, aren't parents and students acting rationally when they seek a prestigious institution (even if it's not a good match), when they accept merit- not need-based scholarships, bargain for aid, and elect a major for its perceived economic value? If by rational we mean to act in ways yielding more money, the answer is yes. Studies reveal that a school's name correlates with later earnings; the major correlates with earnings after graduation. And in a competitive society this behavior is self-reinforcing. As long as hiring and salary decisions are made so categorically, the spiral will steepen: the same studies reveal that it makes no difference how well a student actually performs—only the name on the degree matters (Maull, 1998). This mocks the touted byword *excellence*. There are choices here: actively support or passively accept this system as "rational"; let it increasingly drive applications, admissions, majors, "intellectual" choices, and institutional competition; or question this behavior, create incentives to counter it, even fight it as one that might breed a universal wolf swallowing all else and making the economic instrumentality of education its only good.

This "rational" behavior intensifies in part because higher education is neither regulated nor self-regulated heavily. Governments require accounting procedures, but institutions are free to set salaries, build buildings, target applicants, solicit funds, merge, advertise, outsource, compete, offer varied scholarships and loans, establish branches, invest, specialize, diversify, even monopolize. A market of higher education so unregulated and competitive contains a paradox: many institutions are presumed to pursue the same general ends—intellectual, civic, economic, and idealistic ends that serve learning and society—but many institutions compete against each other in doing so. In order best to serve those larger, shared goals, to what extent should they compete? Or cooperate?

Bart Giamatti became commissioner of baseball for more than love of the game. However different their activities, suggestive similarities exist between professional sports and higher education. Both groups of institutions serve a complex set of national and communal ends—recreative, economic, social, and educational. Both are presumed also to promote larger ideals—the game, sport, values, knowledge, and research. It cannot be the object of one team to drive others out of existence. Beat them on the field, but don't bankrupt them. Yet after the advent of free agency, it became painfully obvious that in those less regulated sports, wealthier teams bought the best players. Those players, often winning a championship, stayed only until better offers came along. Frequently, the team that bought them couldn't afford to keep them. Case in point: the Florida Marlins. Correlation of team wealth and win-loss records is a minor scandal in major league baseball. To combat these inevitable, increasing imbalances, some leagues regulate themselves contractually through salary or payroll caps, guaranteed minimums, unionization and arbitration, rules for drafting and free agency, mandatory sharing of TV revenues to even out major and minor markets, procedures for adding or moving teams, and the power of commissioners beholden to no one team. This serves the health of the sport and is condoned by law. Nothing like this, as far as I know, exists in higher education. (Professional sports lack tenure, but everyone on the roster must be full-time with all fringe benefits.)

If the federal court decision banning schools from sharing financial aid information is any indication—a decision only MIT had the courage to fight—then the courts do not grasp that higher education serves larger, less tangible communal goods as well as individual, tangible interests; that higher education might at least be accorded some options analogous to those open to the dignity of professional sports, such as antitrust exemption (Collis, 1999, pp. 12–13); that education, a unique form of commerce and trade, should be treated uniquely.

Higher education acts as an associative good when it promotes awareness of, and derives benefit from, the lives of others and what they pursue as knowledge, either for its own sake or as a practical instrumentality. Empathy is a hoped-for result; the broader aim should be critical reflection and reasoned discussion, an ideal identified in Renaissance courts, Enlightenment salons, and American colleges by the same word: *conversation.* Learning, then, creates a social and socializing experience, one intensely intellectual when those jostling together are gifted, reflect different backgrounds, and harbor heterogeneous ideas, values, and interests (Hansmann, 1999; Goethals, Winston, and Zimmerman, 1999).

At all levels of learning, knowledge may be pursued for its own sake. If we as a society lose this habit, we shall spend down intellectual capital and fail to replace it. Our capacity to wonder, to be curious, will atrophy. The wellspring of advancement, pure or applied, remains the quest for knowledge as its own end. This is an end or good desired for itself. It is also the final cause of all other goods in the entelechy (Popper, 1962, p. 5).

We soon ask what possible uses that knowledge might or should serve. This questioning is a moral or ethical good. It differs from pursuing knowledge for its own sake; it differs from pursuing it in order to fulfill a particular purpose or to solve certain problems. To ask the possible ramifications of knowledge is a venture not limited to practical questions. Properly speaking, it is philosophical and humane. It forms the basis for organizations such as the Union of Concerned Scientists and Physicians Against Nuclear War. In fact, unlocking the atom offers a series of examples. First came theoretical knowledge sought for its own sake. No one in the early days of nuclear physics worked in order to produce weapons of mass destruction or any other "product"—not Planck, Schrödinger, Bohr, or Einstein. Only later did the exigencies of circumstance and the sophistication of technologies assembled for one purpose permit practical applications: extreme destruction, a problematic source of power, food preservation, medical advances. Each use entails various decisions to implement it or not: deploy the weapon, a political, military, and moral judgment based on values established and debated since before the founding of nation states; irradiate food; build nuclear power plants; use radiation therapy; avoid electromagnetic radiation and its risks. Some decisions override economic incentives.

Genetics presents a similar case. The monk Gregor Mendel did not envision interferon to treat hepatitis. Franklin, Watson, and Crick did not conjure cloned sheep nor trade wars triggered by genetically altered crops. Mendel simply wanted to know why some peas were wrinkled, others smooth; from that he formulated his general laws of heredity. How that knowledge and all it engendered should now be used entails, again, ethical and economic decisions. Though the results of knowledge can be perverted, we cannot prevent abuses before the fact nor predict favorable outcomes. How exactly to use knowledge is rarely a matter of obvious application; it is a long test-essay, not multiple choice—a contest of values, and occasionally a calculated risk. In the humanities, results can be misused, but, more often, the methods and approaches can be trivial, foolish, or twisted by prejudices of all kinds (Bate, 1986, pp. 217–218).

Yet none of this could even be considered if first we did not seek knowledge for its own sake. Specific needs will find specific solutions, but general needs are the hardest to supply. The Promethean spark came before Bessemer furnaces or Frankenstein's creation. An irreducible element in the search for knowledge is the unpredictability of its application.

In education, then—a pale word for that innate drive in the species' quest for answers to the riddles that surround us, existing as we do briefly on a speck of cosmic dust falling through the most tremendous room—first to seek knowledge and ideas for their own sake and then to debate the ethical application of knowledge in an intellectually disinterested fashion are therefore always to be accounted goods in and of themselves.

F. Scott Fitzgerald says that the ability to keep seemingly contradictory ideas simultaneously in one's mind defines intelligence. The entelechy of higher education means several coordinated ends regarded together as producing different kinds of goods. It is both possible and necessary for higher education to serve all these functions; we welcome it as an economically instrumental good, hope for it as an associative intellectual and social good, insist on it as a good in itself—as a final cause—when it seeks for knowledge and ideas for their own sake, and nurture it as a moral good when it investigates, in a disinterested way, the ethical application of knowledge and ideas.

Economic Pressures

But education as an instrumental good geared to competitive gain, coupled with competition among educational institutions, can form a juggernaut threatening to eclipse the other goods and, ironically, subvert its own. To aim only for the instrumental while expecting education to proceed in the general pursuit of knowledge is like expecting a fickle stream constantly to power a mill without first damming it into a pond. To see higher education as primarily an instrumental good—to diminish the pursuit of knowledge sought for its own sake as a self-justifying good and to belittle education as an associative good in the process (who wants to know what someone else is doing if it doesn't contribute to the career you're making?)—is too easily a consequence of following short-term economic "incentives." These will always be linked to practical problems in a technological, capitalistic society whose aim is to create more wealth and to be not only competitive but first. An unregulated, competitive, instrumental economic good seen as the final cause will slowly but surely choke the other goods. Instrumental means—for they are means, not true ends—will be seen as the only end. The entelechy will be destroyed. Young people will find the only attractive, rewarding fields of study are those that meet one or more of three benchmarks: fields that promise (even if the promise is illusory) high wages if pursued as a career; fields that study money; or fields that, within educational institutions themselves, draw money with large grants or gifts.

What if the ideal of knowledge sought for its own sake is devalued, even lost? Several things perish with it. Obviously the possibility of ever converting such knowledge to any practical ends vanishes, a kind of cutting off your nose to spite your face. Aside from examples in nuclear and genetic science, we know thousands of chemical compounds and threatened botanical species whose use remained and or still remains inert until catalyzed by some later mind; if we did not know the properties of the rosy periwinkle of Madagascar we could not preserve the world's most effective treatment for childhood leukemia. The list is endless; many technical applications are unforeseen, some serendipitous.

Another loss is idealism. The best nursery of ideals is the disinterested pursuit of knowledge and ideas and the ethical consideration of how to apply them; to tear down the idealism of learning tears down every ideal.

Another thing threatened if we diminish the free pursuit of ideas, knowledge, and values divorced from maximum economic gain is the attraction of studying different fields of knowledge without first committing to vocational choice. This loss is devastating to any society but particularly to a democracy where freedom to choose and move between jobs or careers is an opportunity inherent to liberty and one contributing to the pursuit of happiness. The effects of this loss won't surface right away; in fact, if everyone learns simply to become more productive, a temporary boost in productivity will result. But within a generation, that approach will deprive any citizenry of perspective, relation, and the ability to connect one field of knowledge with another. We will be forced into ordinary ways of thinking and into predictable, discipline-bound "solutions," exactly what we have stereotypically criticized other nations (not without some reason) for pursuing at the expense of individual initiative and idealism.

All this assumes freedom of choice, essential to democracy. An understanding of several fields is key to such choices because the issues faced by a citizenry asked to decide them through their representatives require that education be an instrumental good for civic and political reasons in a way analogous and allied to, but not identical with, its economic instrumentality. Scholarly debate is, or should be, the standard for a democratic society's procedures of verification and dispute over ideas and policy. If all inquiry serves vested interests and is circumscribed in advance, then in time few inquiries (and none of them controversial) will be pursued to their end. No one fears this outcome more than defenders of a free press. But such political wisdom cannot be achieved by pursuing only economic competition. As Leo Marx, one of the great exponents of American studies in the later twentieth century, states, "The utilitarian idea of the multiversity, and the fragmented . . . conception of knowledge which it favors, are at odds with our presumed commitment to democratic . . . values" (Marx, 1975, p. 12). George Washington realized this political truth when he urged in his farewell address that we "Promote, then, as an object of primary importance, institutions for the general diffusion of knowledge. In proportion as the structure of a government gives force to public opinion, it is essential that public opinion should be enlightened." Education as exclusively an economic instrumental good is characteristic of authoritarian and totalitarian regimes. It coexists comfortably with control of the media, a caste system of jobs, early specialization, even censorship. One egregious example of a turn away from knowledge for its own sake and away from democratic or open ethical deliberation would be China's "cultural" revolution. Intellectuals were driven away from the cities and their books in order to chase birds from seed in the fields. China sabotaged its intellectual capital for two generations. It was the Great Leap Backward.

To repeat, in an ever more competitive world there is a danger that education as an instrumental economic good will attenuate education as an associative intellectual and social good, erode it as a civic good in a free society, diminish it as a moral good, and threaten it as a final good in which knowledge is sought for its own sake. Once the associative, civic, moral, and final goods are enfeebled—and we cannot assume they will thrive on their own without our active help and participation—then education will be a competitive tool bereft of the ability to impart democratic, critical thinking, to transmit cultural values and inheritances, or to discover knowledge with unforeseen, multiple applications. Two related illustrations: the dismissal of Dr. Jerome Kassirer, editor of the *New England Journal of Medicine,* represents, as the Dean of Tufts Medical School, Dr. John

Harrington, puts it, "the triumph of money over medicine." Dr. Kassirer opposed the decision of the board of that journal, the Massachusetts Medical Society, to endorse, for gain, unrelated products and services over which the Journal has no control or oversight. A similar selling out of the *Journal of the American Medical Association* triggered the dismissal of its editor (Tye, 1999).

The keystones in the arch containing the three instrumental and associative goods—economic, social, and civic—are these two goods: the ethical deliberation over how knowledge should be used and the pursuit of knowledge and ideas as an end in itself, which is the final cause. These two goods do not preclude the other goods; foundational, they facilitate them, a fact recognized by every major myth ancient and modern, West and East, whether Plato's cave, the Promethean spark, Pandora's box, the trees of knowledge and of good and evil in Eden, the Faust and Frankenstein myths, or Confucius' idea of *li* and the person educated and disciplined to realize true humanity (*jen*). Knowledge pursued for its own sake and values deliberated in disinterested fashion generate and humanize all the other goods, as well as being potentially complicit in evil misapplications. All great moral and religious systems of the world teach the need to enlighten general knowledge with moral commitment—yet they also recognize the economic, civic, and associative valences of knowledge. But remove the justification of learning pursued as the life of the mind for its own sake and as disinterested ethical deliberation to serve humanity, and all other goods soon will be perverted. For American education to forget this would be tragic hubris. The instrumental goods will become shills for authority without self-criticism and barkers for productivity without cultural inheritance or true curiosity.

Are these warnings moved against money and wealth creation? Not in the least. Like any form of power and exchange—oil, steam, the atom, language, statistics, or human imagination—capital in and of itself is a purely neutral quality of force. It is always better to have more of it rather than less. "To him who hath it shall be given, and to him who hath not even that little he hath shall be taken away." The Twain School of Money sums it up well. When anyone complains, quoting scripture for the purpose, that love of money is the root of evil, think of Twain's remark: "Yes, all money's tainted. Trouble is, 'tain't enough." Yet as every major moralist has affirmed for millennia, it is rather how, how far, and to the exclusion of what else money is pursued that counts; and, once possessed, what one does with it that determines its ethical worth.

Economic prosperity within and outside universities has the potential to insulate institutions from future shocks and constant pressures. It might allow the humanities to flourish on a level not markedly beneath other fields, which is where the humanities are now. Reckoning the last thirty years (especially since 1982), the brute fact is that by every term of prestige and quality measured—faculty salaries, faculty positions created, percentage of adjunct professors, expenditures on physical plant, SAT scores, number of degrees awarded, expansion of high quality graduate programs, and alumni, corporate, and government gifts and grants—the humanities have fallen farther and farther behind (Engell and Dangerfield, 1998). Few educational leaders articulate this fact; fewer urge that anything be done about it. The situation is somewhat cyclical, but the ups and downs transpire while the whole travels downwards; imagine one point on a wheel rolling downhill. Prosperity of the last generation coincides with an overall degradation of the humanities. If we recall the entelechy of higher education, something better could result.

The Problem with Prestige

If any model for organic growth is more than a house of cards, it will prompt change, confirm selected present practices, and merge the two.

Competition and What Counts

Increasingly, we compete for students, money, faculty, endowments, and yield ratios. Competition is a mantra. The contests spin like pinwheels in a fireworks display, faster, brighter, so intense that now the mere reputation of "having" the best rank, the most money, is seemingly what matters, often fixed upon by the media and holding astonishing sway over applicants, parents, even counselors. Bald quantitative scores, amounts, or ranks seem what must be known. These markers possess the power of authenticated status, and measuring them becomes an end in itself (though an earthy Texan might describe these contests with a certain locker room phrase). This obsessive striving overshadows and thus jeopardizes the real ends and goods—scholarly, personal, and social—of the institution. There are no algorithms for complex human behavior, no ranks for distinct entelechies. Excellence, ultimately, cannot be measured or pursued adequately in these often trivialized forms. If it is, it becomes a hollow shell, and if we boast of its counters, we may lose sight of what, supposedly, is being counted. Longinus, echoed by the critic and historian Sainte-Beuve, said it well: nothing so much resembles a hollow as a swelling. Whether *U.S. News & World Report* rankings, yields against the nearest competitor, or endowment building, even as we remark that they are only indicators, we credit them more than we suspect because they have become the only indicators commonly voiced and used. Admittedly they have use, but we need to remind ourselves that they are inherently not intellectual or scholarly; they have nothing to do with the application of learning, they may tend to divide rather than unite the larger community of learning, and they carry no ethical content whatsoever. True symbols of excellence not only mirror excellence, they actually are that quality itself.

Rankings and measures of "excellence" now pursued create status and reputation as final goals or goods in themselves when at best they are shorthand signs of instrumental goods within the institution. But prestige is derived from prestidigitation, "juggler's tricks" in Latin. True reputation comes from knowing and cultivating the thing itself, the institutional entelechy in all its interrelations over a span of time. Metaphorically, more of Peter Lynch's methods of research, investment, and evaluation, and less day trading, quarterly panics, and street rumor would serve us, as educators, better. Henry S. Pritchett, astronomer, later president of MIT and then president of the Carnegie Foundation for Teaching until 1930, in his address to the University of Michigan in 1905, "Shall the University Become a Business Corporation?" praises the democratic spirit of land grant institutions and remarks how they might vie with older ones "in a rivalry [in] which we may well hope to see the noble rivalry of the scholar rather than a rivalry of riches, of buildings, and of numbers." His wisdom is not anachronistic.

The intensification of institutional striving for competitive goals measured by dollars, numbers, or ordinals can whip up heady fixations. It has all the earmarks of addiction. It intensifies itself; more and more of it is required to satisfy the desire; increasing resources drain into it; it distracts us from concrete tasks and personal relations; it makes cooperation difficult; it can prevent larger community; the addiction becomes a burden whose only relief is deeper addiction. Might one renounce, openly and publicly, certain yardsticks as commonly accepted indicators of institutional worth? Or, at least, recall Pritchett's advice, as well as Einstein's: "Not everything that can be counted counts, and not everything that counts can be counted."

Cooperation

Though each school has its unique entelechy, many, at times proximate in location, share larger ideals and aims. As well as competing, they must exploit every chance to unite strengths, cut costs, and serve their communities better. One area where this is happening but must happen much more is libraries. The most common form of grant in the humanities is funding to travel to a research library. An inevitable institutional and economic Darwinism is reducing in this country the number of research libraries considered truly adequate for many fields. So, whether through J-STORE, consortia to share periodical costs (greater than book costs), digital sharing, interlibrary loan, use of the Library of Congress cataloging system, agreements to share faculty and even student patrons, or linking up with public systems, libraries must cooperate or deteriorate. Is it a stretch to carry this to building maintenance, security, athletic facilities, health care bargaining power, and the like? These complex moves, some with legal or labor ramifications, might be impractical at certain schools, but cooperation in higher education, mergers of certain types, if you will, must be vigorously explored.

Leadership and Governance

Organic growth could imply—or from it might be inferred—a slow, predictable process. Such an inference would be myopic. A coming hard freeze requires quick protection; we now know that our most organic form of growth, biological evolution, proceeds at highly uneven rates and responds dramatically to rapid environmental changes or cataclysms, such as massive meteor impacts. Real organic growth encourages institutions to throw off both the addiction to mere status and the inertia of traditional rest; it permits swift executive actions. These ideally are predicated on vertical as well as horizontal consultation, genuinely frank and open. They entail knowing the longer histories of institutional operations (at times overlooked by peripatetic or new administrators or faculty). Then presidents, schools, divisions, even departments must be ready to act, not react, to shed the false conservatism of forms and structures, among them any structures and attitudes of top governance, that can thwart organic change (Collis, 1999, p. 22).

To balance the autocratic and consensual aspects of the university is ever a challenge. However, the new complexity and regulations universally agreed to that have characterized the last twenty to thirty years will, if not dealt with boldly, continue to grow entirely on their own, internally, without any new addition; this bureaucratic growth will quash both autocratic and democratic strains of governance. (Parkinson's Law, a serious, statistical study of office-running aspects of the British Empire, makes instructive reading applied to universities.) Leaders will feel like Gulliver tied down in Lilliput; faculty, students, and staff will feel like pawns in a Kafka novel. Can we cite anyone who demonstrates that all or even the majority of growth in academic administration and staff is attributable to government regulation and external requirements? (I have searched and cannot.) Gardens need vigorous weeding—often.

The split between administration and faculty, between "advancement" and "academic" leaders, seems to be deepening. This endangers the entelechy of higher education as a whole. Fewer experienced professors seem trained or inclined to administer whole institutions or significant aspects of them; more administrators build careers on managing the essential undertakings and appurtenances of scholarship and teaching rather than participating directly in them for a decade or two. Can we not work from both ends: identify, cultivate, and train faculty as administrators above the departmental level; increase the faculty willing to serve, full- or part-time, for specified periods, in administrative roles; seek career administrators with a demonstrably successful span of teaching or research, not just a line on the resume?

The entelechy of an institution should be reflected in its trustees and governing boards. At that level, Pritchett warns against "administration of experts by [educational] experts." He goes on to say that perhaps no "wiser councilor" exists than a businessperson "of large sympathy and of real interest in intellectual problems." The last quality is paramount. Admittedly, these people "are almost as difficult to find as are great teachers" (Pritchett, 1905, p. 297b). But we must find them, and they should abjure the habit, which some practice, of measuring the success of their chief executive officer (a title used by Pritchett as early as 1905) in purely quantitative ways—how much money raised, how many square feet added, what rank achieved? It might be prudent to consider having on these boards at least one faculty member from another institution, one whose interest in organization and management complements the interest in intellectual problems felt by nonacademics on the board. In many cases, trustees meet too infrequently and go into too little detail to be of real help in effecting organic change. Instead, we get lapses, then lurches.

Academic Planning and Curriculum

Organic growth in an era of rapid change demands intensified strategic, long-term academic planning charted by faculty and administrators working closely together on a regular basis, not sporadically or prompted by an upcoming campaign or crisis only. These groups need to be provided with applicable national literature and studies relevant to their tasks, not (what happens all too often) just information gathered internally and reports authored at the institution.

It is desirable to create at the interdepartmental, even the interschool level, permanent rather than ad hoc groups whose sole task is to develop courses and programs that push academic administrative and disciplinary boundaries, either through team teaching, inherently interdisciplinary fields, or both (for example, the environment, human rights, science, and public policy). These groups of faculty and administrators might suggest changes in academic administrative structures themselves as well as in curricula and courses.

In search procedures and hiring, faculty (even administrators) can conduct themselves in counterproductive, amateurish, even unprofessional ways that betray the entelechy of goods that hiring the best possible person is meant to further (Stein and Trachtenberg, 1993). I can confirm this from personal witness, reports of graduate students on the market, and tales from colleagues. Every professor should be versed—through seminars, meetings, reading, or all of them—on the ground rules, assignments, realistic expectations, activities, advertising, interviewing, prohibitions, and negotiations of the process. Professors in general seem not well trained in hiring. They often do not have time for this long, arduous process. Their efforts may become permanent mistakes that everyone suffers.

Higher education has not escaped the passion for celebrity and name recognition in our society of rapid change and media exposure. In the humanities and social sciences, "star" quality may seem obvious but is, in fact, very hard to determine and often illusory. In those fields especially, more than ever subject to trends, factions, and fashions with short half-lives, informed opinion varies, and to fix on one name rarely furthers organic growth. Sometimes a "star" catches the crest of a wave that has already broken; there is less consensus about who is a "star" than a generation ago. Some "stars" shamelessly milk the system. They count on administrative timidity, on fear of seeming to have failed to bag the quarry, and they frequently waste everyone's time—and money. Relative equity is not flashy, but organic growth requires attention to it. The hierarchical commodification and segmenting of the professoriate within fields and also between fields harbors perils. If the market is followed fatalistically or constantly trumped, rather than to some degree resisted on principle, the market will become tyrannical, leave no options, and make some jobs and fields so relatively unappealing to the young that few talents will want to enter them.

The resort to adjunct and part-time faculty, after having doubled in the last twenty years, may have bottomed out. It should. Institutions such as Georgia State University are showing the way to more sane, long-term, organic policies: carefully create full-time posts, cultivate the young professionally, commit resources, and two academic generations from now the school will be stronger, its faculty more committed and loyal with higher morale. Few adjuncts are pleased with their situation. How embittered, resentful, and desperate some feel is hard to gauge only because the feelings run so deep. A disaffected teaching force cannot and will not work to help an institution grow or change. Reducing reliance on piecework teaching in no way precludes strenuous, periodic reviews of tenured as well as untenured faculty.

Our oldest piece of electronic communication technology (save the telegraph) seems vastly underused. McGeorge Bundy employed it all the time, to great effect, as Harvard's dean from 1954 to 1960. James Baker, running George Bush's campaign, made dozens of calls each day. But in our crush of formal committees, conferences, councils, and engagements, usually segregated into separate "administration" and "academic" buildings, we rarely, faculty or administrators, telephone and ask, "What are your chief concerns? Please be candid." Individual faculty can feel, even cynically, that the layers between them and key administrators are tall barriers. These barriers—as much when they are only perceived to exist as when they actually do—block growth and change more than we think. What a difference it makes for a dean or provost to call, to cultivate, in informal, private conversations, both intelligent gossip and bedrock opinion, perhaps dispelling rumors on the way. This is not unseemly. Most faculty welcome it; some crave it. With word processors and e-mail, perhaps losing the art of dictation was inevitable. But losing the art of informal conversation between administration and faculty cuts the internal sympathetic nervous system.

Student Life, Advising, and Attitudes

Students need to know the history and entelechy of their own institution, as do faculty. A few paragraphs in a handbook won't do. If there is no recent detailed account, someone in history or a keen alumnus or alumna might write one, if not as a book then as a substantial pamphlet that could also be disseminated digitally. (This would be both scholarship and service.) We might consider offering, even requiring, a short course in American higher education and its history. Of the wealth of material here, much of it recent and well written, most students, incredibly, never read a word—they are not asked to—and only schools of education deign to pick it up. Students are entering "higher education" and should acquire some sense of the entire enterprise, but to most of them it is just a blur. If a requirement for this seems outlandish, perhaps a seminar or series of presentations during freshman week or orientation would not. A section of the bookstore devoted to higher education, to publications on or about the institution, and by people affiliated with it, might be a focal point.

Business and community leaders, journalists, artists, lawyers, physicians, heads of nonprofits—all the better if alumni—can speak about the importance of academic life personally, what it meant and means to them, how they continue intellectual interests and avocations, what opportunities they missed, what new paths were opened (this reverses the all too common, though not intrinsically bad, habit of getting them to talk about their present professions).

Students need advising not only to fill out course registrations but as young adults benefiting from an older adult who gets them to probe more deeply their own motives for shaping their own most fundamental curricular choices and, more than that, for shaping years of their own lives—even, perhaps especially, if they are part-time students. It's not enough to check requirements, achieve "balance," and ponder different courses. Most students secretly desire—and they always need—serious conversations about the aims and ends of their education and the direction of their lives as a whole. Once a term is not enough. Ten minutes is not enough. How a student conceives of and fits into the entelechy, pursuing instrumental, associative, and final goods, can form one general template for these conversations. One aim of advising is for the student to develop a grounded sense of hope, the hope to be a better person for experiencing higher education, and to know why; the hope to contribute to some project greater than the individual self, a goal that can harness and subordinate, rather than succumb to or deny, the range of motives for personal success or gain.

We might talk more openly, directly, and publicly about student life than we do. This is not to advocate a return to all kinds of rules. But our policy statements and disciplinary procedures seem insufficient and impersonal. They have all the force and all the impotence of abstract catechisms. The recent Binge Beer newspaper "ad" signed by over a hundred college presidents is a welcome tactic, and one of the best things any administration can do is to set a tone, an expectation. Yet a tone is set chiefly by personal acts of commission and is best set orally, or face to face, not through anonymous policies.

Students rarely examine the academic work of other students; it is virtually "uncool" to do so. Institutions can publicize and insure outlets for this work. Prizes do this, but not well. A better, more consistent and more equitable way is to support publications (print or electronic) that describe or reproduce, with permission, student projects, essays, papers, or experiments, integrating them into teaching wherever possible. Peer effects should at times take effect through the published forms of communication actually used by a community of scholars.

Open forums, even debates, involving students, faculty, administrators, and guests (the mix is key) may seem needlessly to court controversy, but they leverage the presence of the institution to expose and train students in mature deliberation, persuasion, and different points of view. If controversy threatens free speech violations or intimidation, these can be adjudicated if firm rules and publicized procedures are in place.

The Humanities

How have the humanities themselves reacted to accelerating change, competition, technology, and pressures? Too often they have reacted in self-involved, self-defeating ways. A few humanists stuck their heads in the sand and waited for change to go away. Others fell upon each other in accusations of right and left, traditional and enlightened, canonical and liberating. This produced some positive curricular changes and aired cultural questions. It elicited some lamentable changes too. The debates were not always responsible in scholarly terms; divisions left many embittered. Demographic and theoretical developments of the 1970s and 1980s altered humanistic disciplines, especially the modern languages, but the humanities had little impact on the way higher education views or governs itself. As in certain undistinguished periods of the past, some humanists wrote prose that even few other humanists could understand. Without grasping either the principles of modern science or the history of philosophy, some fell upon any claim to objectivity or truth in any field. The idea of disinterestedness came under attack. Many humanists urged, and taught, that we are all interested in our own ideologies, and then, either explicitly or implicitly, claimed that this applies equally across the board. The ideal of being disinterested became just another "ideology," equally suspect. Troubling, too, was one general failure (might it be called ignorance?) of humanists who "discovered" being "interdisciplinary" or, conversely, pursued hyperspecialization. Both groups failed to grasp that, historically (no matter what narrowing had occurred since the 1940s), the humanities had always sought results emanating from other areas of endeavor in order to incorporate those results into judgments of human value, relevance, and historical significance. This is one aspect of Matthew Arnold's apologia: the humanities absorb and interpret the results of science, knowledge, and technology for our inner lives, values, and ideals. The humanities help direct their uses in light of what we inherit in our cultures, in light of what we cherish yet also criticize, in light of what we must change in order to continue to cherish.

The humanities can better meet our current predicaments if they

- Teach rhetoric and prose argument again, not simply as the correction of mechanical faults in composition, but as logic, dialectic, and persuasion; that is, teach language as that great instrumentality serving all nonquantitative disciplines. In order to do this we must use excellent models of intellectual prose, the vast majority of which are not contemporary; we should stop teaching composition as autobiography and improve the textbooks for it
- Teach what always in the Western tradition accompanied rhetoric (partly because some philosophers viewed rhetoric dimly), that is, moral philosophy, and do so prior to teaching any professional ethics (it is too late then to start)
- Teach the study of religion—not belief in any religion proper but a comparative grasp of the world's great value systems, which have profoundly religious bases (this is beginning, prompted by new textbooks and new attitudes)
- Seek relevance from the past, not in showy ways, forcing Austen or Shakespeare to be "our contemporary," but challenging us to ask why certain texts and arts persist, why we find in them ideas and visions that do not die and are not mired in the prejudices of their own times. ("Relevance," tainted by its use in the 1960s, has always been one goal of the humanities: affect action and conduct. As Whitehead says, the danger of academic study is inert knowledge. Burke argues that, accounting for changed circumstances but not jettisoning wisdom, past models should not be directly imitated but imaginatively applied.)

- Insist on interdisciplinary study rather than talk about it (for example, no Ph.D. program in English that I know of requires formal study in history, history of science, philosophy, government, or religion; languages required have slipped from three to, sometimes, one). In short, revitalize *literae humaniores*, the articulated spine of many disciplines that form the backbone of the humanities—plural
- Ask, in teaching, publication, and promotions, how specialization serves general humanistic ends.

We now have more of past and present expressions of human experience available to us than ever. We have the potential to produce educated individuals who are the least provincial in history. Technology is an added boon. Information systems are sophisticated enough to benefit the humanities. They are revolutionizing libraries and can spread humanistic learning as nothing else since the rise of mass literacy and the printed book. Vast collections are at our fingertips (all English poetry and much prose, from 800 to 1900, for example). "Colleges and universities will be increasingly interested in maintaining an attractive technology environment as the competition for students grows more intense" (Lau, 1999). Without sacrificing traditional print collections and face-to-face conversation and contact, this must become true in the humanities too.

A caveat. Since 1650—Milton being the most recent plausible candidate to have read virtually all that was printed in his own day—there have always existed more key texts and scholarship in the humanities (now even in a single subfield) than any one person can consult, let alone master. The crucial issue is actual time spent in hard reading, careful listening, and painstaking revision. Only 15 percent of college papers are rewritten (*Chronicle of Higher Education*, 1999). The technology having greatest impact on American society since 1950 may still well be TV. Two separate studies cited by *Time* (August 16, 1999, p. 21) provide sobering statistics: the average American child views 30,000 TV commercials per year, estimated conservatively at 35 minutes each day; the average child aged six to twelve reads 63.7 hours per year at home (11 minutes each day), one-third the time spent viewing commercials, let alone the actual programs. Recall the halcyon predictions from education experts in the early 1950s about the virtually limitless, positive effects of TV? The sad irony is they had good reasons to make them.

Because much of the humanities' subject matter was written in, or deals with, times before the present generation, it is often assumed that the humanities look essentially backward, concerned with the human condition as it has been rather than as it is or might be. Even someone as sophisticated as Harold Shapiro can regard humanistic education as having stressed mere "indoctrination," and "some specified set of moral claims" (Shapiro, 1997, pp. 78–79), a judgment that would have disturbed not a few thinkers venerated in older pantheons: Socrates, for instance, or Erasmus, Mary Wollstonecraft, Samuel Johnson, François Voltaire, Immanuel Kant, John Quincy Adams, George Eliot, or Frederick Douglass. It has been the province of the humanities to preserve in order to reform, to pay attention, even homage, to the past, but to criticize what we inherit, calibrating the fact that social and individual lives change in the present, and that the education of character, the shaping of society, balance what has been known with the pressure of what is discovered. The humanities openly cherish and brazenly criticize and see no contradiction in the two.

Of the implications and actions suggested in this section, some may seem old hat, others doubtful, a few minor; but each stems from a vision of the whole institutional enterprise and the coordination of its constituent parts. Organic growth is as complex as the change that influences it, but it cannot be merely reactive. It will work best if it cleaves to principles and goods best grasped as an entelechy whose formulation itself is not permanent but self-evolving.

Rapid Change, Long Views

There is no Golden Age good enough to want to return to. Nostalgia in that regard cheapens history. But the metamorphosis of ideals, the transformation and creation of ideas, the alliance between civic and educational areas, and the realignment of the universe of knowledges—none of this can take place imaginatively without knowing what those knowledges have been and what purposes they and their institutions have served, for society and for individual Bildung. Only by knowing the past—including the past of our own institutions—can one anticipate the ways in which organic change might best take place. Constitutional scholars and judges know this. Economic market analysis and risk-taking exemplify it. This knowledge at times is quantitative or experimental; in human institutions it must be expressed and practiced in assimilative, complex ways, quantitatively and qualitatively, the result of which is the capacity to make decisions about people, goals, and motivations, integrating them with decisions about dollars and bytes. Jaroslav Pelikan has studied with care the history of American education. He concludes: "The most successful leaders of modern universities have been those who have come to their task from the 'business' of teaching and research, but have then learned to administer the university as 'business' without being overwhelmed by it" (Pelikan, 1992, p. 72). In other words, the ends are known and practiced first; then institutional means are mastered and fitted to those ends.

An organic model is not from technology or science, nor from economic and social fields, nor from the separate disciplines in the humanities as we have come to practice them. The model—a distinction with a difference—is broadly humanistic. That broad humanism differs from the usual methods in individual academic disciplines in the humanities, a difference as great as that between the humanities and the sciences or technology. No one discipline can claim superiority of contribution. The idea must come from the whole person, hence the continued importance of liberal education, of the liberal arts and sciences, as a goal in itself and as a foundation for any professional expertise. The premise of organic change, then, is not from "the humanities" in the usual sense; it is humanistic in a larger sense. It does not require someone trained in the humanities to act in this regard as a humanist. And the disciplines that forget this fact most often are the humanities themselves. This is true especially when they trivialize or defend themselves, well, defensively. It will prove wiser to see knowledge and reason and the forms of them "we employ in the various 'humanities'" as "basically a public inheritance" (Peters, 1975, p. 149). We are all, in David Hume's phrase, of the party of humanity.

Our national union, our universities and colleges, too, serve society not only with due weight to each individual but with a view to integration. This sense of *architektonik*—of varied activities and knowledges emerging organically through time in interrelated worth as they impinge on human conduct, academies, and civil societies—was once the province of a discipline regarded as consummate. From Plato through Augustine, from Sidney to Kant, this vision was the province of philosophy. (A reminder is the highest degree in arts or sciences, no matter the field, *philosophiae doctoris*.) Its continuation is found in, among others, Schelling, Hegel, Humboldt, and Cardinal Newman, moving spirits of modern universities at Jena, Berlin, Dublin, and elsewhere. This is not the place for an excursus, but we could trace this conviction, too, in the writings and actions of Jefferson, Washington, Lee, Lincoln, Howard and the Freedman's Bureau, in de Clare, the Wadhams, and the Sidgwicks—all associated with learning at particular colleges or universities.

It must be admitted that this philosophical sense is practiced rarely and taught almost never, perhaps because such a large vision of knowledge, values, and intellectual virtue is not specialized. It cannot be specialized. Anything this important is too important to leave to the specialist mind. The university is an organism with specialized parts, but essentially one body, and it can act as such. Its different parts should not be like walls and gates that separate and imprison, but, as Francis Bacon said, like veins and arteries that connect the larger body of knowledge and its applications.

Universities exist both within and outside what Wordsworth calls the world of "getting and spending." They must continue to enjoy a special status and relationship with society. We do not want an ivory tower, nor do we want business offices masquerading as a campus. If we need an image, let it be a lighthouse permitting the commerce of ideas and knowledge and preventing their foundering or destruction. And we want that lighthouse, or rather those lighthouses, to work as lighthouses do, impartially but visibly and dependably, over long periods of time for the good of all, as beacons that permit discovery of new territories. Their permeable border with immediate social and economic needs must yet be maintained as a border, a clear independence (Barber, 1989, p. 66; Kennedy, 1997, p. 15). We are all tacit shareholders in every institution of learning. No one, except a wrecker, wants to see any lighthouse fail, especially not another lighthouse keeper.

We must take long views, longer even than those views demanded by financial investments. This is not for our generation alone; it is for a common, not an exclusive, posterity. For the success of this long view the bottom line is not the best metaphor. Ending his chapter "Change From Without" in *Education's Great Amnesia,* Robert Proctor explores this metaphor and concludes starkly: "The past can have little or no meaning in a society ruled by the bottom line" (Proctor, 1988, pp. 138–139). Yet that metaphor is far from the worst. Mr. Micawber is right about budgets. Income twenty pounds, expenses nineteen pounds, nineteen shillings, sixpence; result: happiness. Income twenty pounds, expenses twenty pounds and sixpence; result: misery. The yearly budget and five-year capital campaign are tools, means to crucial ends. They further the entelechy but are not the entelechy itself.

Any institution encompassing these means and ends by its own specific formulation of them must recognize their interplay in a society in which we all have a stake, in which we attempt to create a more perfect union, the entelechy, if you will, of civic polity, the pattern of which is our Constitution, one that, with its amendments and carefully deliberated motto, *e pluribus unum,* is a political model for organic growth. With its built-in capacity to meet change as interpreted through the generations, that Constitution aims not only in positive terms to establish government, it limits tyranny, balances the whole with the parts, prevents one area or region from swallowing the others, and promotes the general welfare. It aims to admit change but not without check and consent. It works more slowly, thank goodness, than other institutions or corporations. Colleges and universities, like the Constitution, live on a long wavelength. They consist of, and persist in, purposes that should be grasped organically as an entelechy of means, ends, and goods, of causes both immediate and final. If institutions of higher education do not resolve to make every effort to grow through their own principles of organic change, if they do not seek, reexamine constantly, and strive to maintain their own entelechy, then accelerating change will force them to become organizations whose operations and very existence are dictated from without rather than directed from within.

References

Axtell, J. *The Pleasures of Academe: A Celebration and Defense of Higher Education.* Lincoln: University of Nebraska Press, 1998.

Barber, B. "The Civic Mission of the University." *Kettering Review,* Fall 1989.

Bate, W. J. Interview by J. P. Russo. In R. J. Barth and J. L. Mahoney (eds.), *Coleridge, Keats, and the Imagination.* Columbia: University of Missouri Press, 1986.

Chronicle of Higher Education, Aug. 1999.

Collis, D. J. "When Industries Change: Scenarios for Higher Education." In M. E. Devlin and J. W. Meyerson (eds.), *Forum Futures: 1999 Papers.* New Haven, Conn.: Forum Publishing, 1999.

Devlin, M. E., "Fast Foreword." In M. E. Devlin and J. W. Meyerson (eds.), *Forum Futures: 1999 Papers.* New Haven, Conn.: Forum Publishing, 1999.

Engell, J. and Dangerfield, A. "Humanities in the Age of Money: The Market-Model University," *Harvard Magazine,* 1998 (May/June), pp. 48–55, 111.

Goethals, G., Winston, G., and Zimmerman, D. "Students Educating Students: The Emerging Role of Peer Effects in Higher Education." In M. E. Devlin and J. W. Meyerson (eds.), *Futures Forum: 1999 Papers.* New Haven, Conn.: Forum Publishing, 1999.

Hansmann, H. "Higher Education as an Associative Good." In M. E. Devlin and J. W. Meyerson (eds.), *Futures Forum: 1999 Papers.* New Haven, Conn.: Forum Publishing, 1999.

Kennedy, D. *Academic Duty.* Cambridge, Mass.: Harvard University Press, 1997.

Lapham, L. *Money and Class in America: Notes and Observations on Our Civil Religion.* New York: Weidenfeld & Nicolson, 1988.

Lau, S. Quoted in "Fast Track: Education, Colleges Spent $3.1B on IT Products in 1998." *Boston Globe,* August 29, 1999, p. D4.

Marx, L. "Technology and the Study of Man." In R. W. Niblett (ed.), *The Sciences, the Humanities, and the Technological Threat.* London: University of London Press, 1975.

Maull, N. Unpublished paper delivered at the Paris Conference on Comparative International Higher Education, 1998.

Pelikan, J. *The Idea of the University: A Reexamination.* New Haven, Conn.: Yale University Press, 1992.

Peters, R. S. "Subjectivity and Standards." In R. W. Niblett (ed.), *The Sciences, the Humanities, and the Technological Threat.* London: University of London Press, 1975.

Popper, K. R. *The Open Society and Its Enemies.* Vol. 2: *The High Tide of Prophecy: Hegel, Marx, and the Aftermath.* New York: Harper & Row, 1962.

Pritchett, H. S. "Shall the University Become a Business Corporation," *Atlantic Monthly,* 1905, 96(3), 289–299.

Proctor, R. *Education's Great Amnesia.* Princeton, N.J.: Association of American University Presses, 1988.

Shapiro, H. "Cognition, Character, and Culture in Undergraduate Education: Rhetoric and Reality." In R. G. Ehrenberg (ed.), *The American University: National Treasure or Endangered Species?* Ithaca, N.Y.: Cornell University Press, 1997.

Smith, H. *Rethinking America.* New York: Random House, 1995.

Stein, R. H. and Trachtenberg, S. J. *The Art of Hiring in America's Colleges and Universities.* Buffalo, N.Y.: Prometheus Books, 1993.

Taylor, J. *Circus of Ambition: The Culture of Wealth and Power in the Eighties.* New York: Warner Books, 1989.

Time, August 16, 1999, p. 21.

Tye, L. Quoted in *International Herald Tribune* [Larry Tye, *The Boston Globe*], July 27, 1999, p. 4.

Wilson, W. "What Is a College For?" *Scribner's Magazine,* 1909, XLVI (July–December), 570–577.

PART TWO

DEFINING AND MANAGING COSTS

CHAPTER FOUR

MAINTAINING A NICE GREEN LAWN

The Competitive Landscape in Lower Profile College Sports

James L. Shulman, William G. Bowen

Shulman and Bowen consider the effects of competitive pressures in "lower profile" college sports; that is, all sports other than football, men's basketball, and men's ice hockey. They examine the financial costs of such sports and the academic qualifications of athletes participating in them. Their data indicate that the level at which institutions choose to compete has a significant impact on both financial and academic matters. As an institution's competitive level increases, costs rise and, on average, athletes' SAT scores decline. The authors urge review of the role of athletics on college campuses in light of clear and accurate financial data and a strong sense of institutional mission.

[Warned of water shortages,] we are far better off if we all . . . let the lawns get a little browner.

A homeowner, stepping onto his back porch at night, cocks his head and hears the swish of invisible lawn sprinklers in the darkness up and down the block. He damns the lack of enforcement and turns the handle on his own sprinkler, making the violation unanimous.

SCHELLING (1978)

This chapter draws heavily from the research presented in *The Game of Life: College Sports and Educational Values* (2001). We are grateful to the Princeton University Press for permission to publish this material. We also would like to express our gratitude to our collaborators on that book, Lauren Meserve and Roger Schonfeld, as well as to three researchers whose suggestions and generous conversation have been extremely important to the development of this article: Mike McPherson, Morty Schapiro, and Gordon Winston.

Tom Schelling's tale reminds us that we sometimes find ourselves in the position of doing something to make ourselves slightly better off and, in doing so, contribute to the whole system being worse off. *Someone* on the street cares enough about his or her garden to break the rule and turn on the sprinklers, leading to a retaliatory strike by others, and eventually by everybody. Under the normal presumption of a social contract, Schelling notes, "Some gain more than others, and some not enough to compensate for what they give up." And soon the well will inevitably go dry. In this article, we describe how this process plays out when one college (or admissions officer, dean, coach, or trustee) cares a great deal about lacrosse, swimming, or squash.

As colleges and universities compete to attract students, faculty, and donations, they are often caught up in a race of what economist Gordon Winston refers to as "competing amenities." If Vanderbilt learns that a student chose to attend Duke over Vanderbilt because of the beautiful tulips on Duke's campus, the order immediately goes out for bulbs at Vanderbilt. In this essay, we examine the institutional repercussions of the competition in sports that take place far from the football stadium, the basketball court, or the hockey rink; that is to say, we ask what competing in sports costs when there are no delusions of gate or TV revenue, when few alumni are watching, and when it is hard to see how the sport affects many people besides those who are participating.

The Schelling sprinkler analogy is helpful for thinking about the competition in these sports in two ways. First, in the same way that the water users do not believe that they are, individually, going to make much of a difference by turning on the faucet, so also trying to get ahead of the pack in these sports is perceived to have little financial or curricular impact on the schools that are trying to get ahead. This may be the case, or it may be the case that the collective repercussions of small incremental turns of a faucet eventually lead to changes of some significance.

The Schelling sprinkler analogy fails, however, to capture an important element of the landscape of college sports. In the sprinkler example, the drought will eventually end, the summer will pass, or the city will run out of water and the citizens will, perhaps, learn their lesson. But in sports the cycles do not end. The fall season leads to the winter and spring, and eventually to the next fall. New sports can be added, talent levels increased, and better coaches found. Even winning a championship does not lead to any rest, since there is always a new season for which to prepare. If, as we posited above, turning the faucet is considered to have only incidental impact, then this endless cycle of opportunities to compete is also considered to be harmless. If there are costs, however, the endless arenas for competition must inevitably magnify those costs.

Schools now must compete not only on the field but also in the quality of their sports facilities. In February of 1997, Yale hired Marisa Didio, the field hockey coach who had left Division I-A Northwestern after making the Final Four: "Within the support system that existed, I did not feel that I could take that [Northwestern] team any further. . . . Yale has made a change in commitment with this hire to bring the program, within a time frame, to another level." At the time that Didio was hired, the Harvard coach explained one aspect of the competitive disadvantage that Yale had been facing: "Certainly, a higher level of field hockey is played on astroturf. Princeton got turf two years ago and that turned their program around. Turf helps in recruiting and in developing team skills. It makes a huge difference."

In this chapter, we begin by looking at the financial costs of lower profile sports, using publicly available data, as well as considering some of the financial investments that are often overlooked. We then turn to trends in the SAT scores of athletes who play such sports as a result of the competition for talented athletes. Finally, we conclude by "thinking out loud" about the implications of this unusual model of competition.

Away from the Spotlight: Lower Profile Sports

In *The Game of Life: College Sports and Educational Values*, we examine a broader set of issues related to college sports. In this chapter, we examine only certain aspects of what we call "lower profile" sports—all sports other than football, men's basketball, and men's ice hockey—at selective colleges and universities, ranging from Swarthmore and Kenyon, to Ivy League universities like Yale and Columbia, to big-time universities like Stanford and the University of Michigan. Few would argue that these sports have a direct impact on the revenues that are earned by a school, in the same way that high-profile sports like football and basketball do. But the competition among schools in these sports is, nevertheless, intense, and it is interesting to note that at the schools in this study, there are twice as many lower profile athletes among the men than there are football, basketball, and hockey players combined; 12 percent of the men at the schools in the study played sports ranging from baseball to fencing, and tennis to soccer, while 6 percent of the men played the three more highly visible sports.

We make use of the Equity in Athletics Disclosure Act (EADA) filings that each of the schools makes available in order to understand the financial sides of the equation; we also draw on a restricted access database called College and Beyond that contains individual student records pertaining to those students who entered thirty selective colleges and universities in 1951, 1976, and 1989.[1]

Financial Investments

We begin the analysis by categorizing the institutions for whom we have dependable data by the scope of their athletic programs. There are enough similarities between types of intercollegiate programs to permit us to group most of the College and Beyond institutions into four categories:[2]

- *Division I-A "Plus" Universities.* The four Division I-A universities in our database that have the most ambitious intercollegiate programs and spend the most money on them (University of Michigan, Penn State, Notre Dame, and Stanford).
- *Division I-A "Standard" Universities.* The four other Division I-A universities in our database that also have big-time programs but that generally enroll somewhat fewer athletes and spend somewhat less money on intercollegiate sports (Duke, Northwestern, Vanderbilt, and Tulane).
- *Division I Ivy League Universities.* The four Ivy League schools in the database (Columbia, University of Pennsylvania, Princeton, and Yale).
- *Division III Coed Liberal Arts Colleges.* The seven coeducational liberal arts colleges in the database (Denison, Kenyon, Hamilton, Oberlin, Swarthmore, Wesleyan, and Williams).

The institutional investments in lower profile sports are far from trivial, ranging from total annual outlays averaging $10 million per school in the Division I-A Plus category, to an average of $5.7 million per school in Division I-A Standard, to averages of $3.5 million per school in the Ivies, and just over $800,000 among the Division III liberal arts colleges. The large difference in outlays on lower profile sports between the Division I-A Plus and the I-A Standard schools is almost entirely explainable in terms of differences in the breadth of athletic offerings (with the Division I-A Plus schools fielding an average of twenty-three teams as compared with an average of fourteen in the Division I-A Standard category). The Ivy League schools, on the other hand, field twice as many teams as we find in the Division I-A Standard schools but spend only about 60 percent as much money on them.

Clearly there are large differences in average spending per team (Figure 4.1), with the two groups of Division I-A schools spending an average of more than $400,000 on each lower profile team, as compared with averages of $126,000 in the Ivy League and $42,000 in the Division III colleges. These large differences demonstrate—even outside the arena of big-time football and men's basketball—

Figure 4.1. Expenditures on Average, Lower Profile Teams (in thousands)

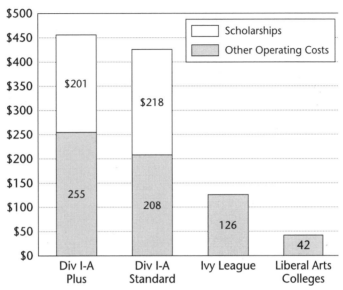

Source: Equity in Athletics Disclosure Act data 1997–98 and Appendix Table 11.1.[3]

the financial impact of the chosen level of play. The Division I-A universities spend nearly *ten times* as much per team (and per athlete) as the Division III colleges, and the Ivies spend *three times* as much per team as their Division III brethren.

Moreover, this pattern is quite consistent when we make comparisons on a sport-by-sport basis for both men's and women's teams. The leading exception to this rule is women's basketball, which is on the way to becoming a big-time sport and shows a more pronounced set of differences in outlays by division. The Division I-A universities spend an average of about $1 million per year on their women's basketball teams, whereas the Ivies spend perhaps $225,000, and the Division III colleges about $40,000.[4]

The most interesting comparisons involve the other lower profile sports. We were able to collect detailed expenditure data for representative schools in each division for field hockey, tennis (men's and women's), swimming (men's and women's), men's soccer, and men's lacrosse. The similarities in expenditures within divisions are pronounced. At the Division I-A level, the average outlay per sport for the sports listed above was in the range of $300,000 to $375,000 per year. In the Ivy League, the average outlay was in the $110,000 to $135,000 range, and in Division III it was consistently in the $30,000 to $50,000 range. Men's lacrosse is a relatively expensive sport, while tennis (for both men and women) is relatively inexpensive, but the variations by sport are not large.

The differences by division, on the other hand, are striking. They are driven, first, by the large number of athletic scholarships given to athletes playing lower profile sports in Division I-A and especially by the scholarships given to women athletes in an effort to balance the heavy spending on football scholarships for men. Of course, many of the men playing lower profile sports at these schools also receive athletically related student aid. We estimate that about half the difference between the Ivies and the Division I-A schools in expenditures on lower profile sports is due to the awarding of athletic scholarships (with the other half due to a combination of factors listed later in the chapter). This use of athletic scholarships is a clear example of "contagion" effects. Patterns established in big-time sports at Division I-A schools spread more or less inexorably to other sports. Returning to the Schelling image, we realize that lawn care is something we all understand regardless of the size of our garden; if someone's twenty acres are lush, you don't feel that it's just fine for your tiny front yard to be ragged. When information flows freely, expectations rise to a highest common denominator.

Staffing Costs

We see this same phenomenon, albeit in slightly muted form, in staffing arrangements, which are the second main determinant of divisional differences in outlays in the lower profile sports. In this regard, the Ivies have much more in common with the Division I-A schools than they do with the liberal arts colleges that compete in Division III. In both the Division I-A schools and the Ivy League, the common pattern is for the head coaches of most lower profile sports to be assigned full-time to their sports. This is the reason why coaching costs, as best we can estimate them, differ less than one might have expected as one moves across the divide between Division I-A and the Ivies. For example, we estimate that coaching costs (excluding benefits) in field hockey range from a high of $128,000 at one Division I-A school to a low of $60,000 at one of the Ivies, with the figures for all of the other schools for which we have data in the $62,000 to $72,000 range. In sharp contrast, coaching outlays for field hockey in the Division III schools for which we have comparable data are around $20,000. Almost identical patterns exist in tennis.

As was noted in our earlier discussion of football and men's basketball, the Division III schools continue to expect most of their coaches to perform a variety of coaching, teaching, and administrative tasks, and the cost savings are both direct and indirect. A very few highly successful Ivy League teams are also coached by individuals who have a variety of duties (an example is Al Carlson at Columbia, who is head coach of golf part-time and associate director of athletics), but the trend is clearly in the direction of dedication to a particular sport. The only other part-time head coach at Columbia coaches archery.

The presence of full-time coaches makes possible aggressive off-campus recruiting and greater commitments to off-season conditioning and preparation of athletes than would otherwise be feasible. Other expenses of all kinds (especially for equipment and travel, as well as recruiting trips and visits) rise accordingly, and this is why the Ivies spend nearly three times as much per lower profile sport as the Division III colleges. Even when we correct for the fact that there tend to be somewhat more athletes per team in the Ivies than in Division III, we find that total expenditures per lower profile athlete in the Ivies are appreciably greater than in Division III—roughly $4,000 in the Ivies versus $1,500 in Division III. Of course, the Ivies regularly compete with Division I-A schools for national championships in sports such as lacrosse, crew, and field hockey, and so this level of expenditure is not really surprising when seen in the context of ambitions for success at the highest levels of play. And if the Ivies are going to compete for coaches and the best athletes with their Division I-A counterparts, they are naturally going to feel the pressure to offer reasonably comparable programs (with the exception of athletic scholarships), including similar schedules, travel, and facilities.[5]

Capital Costs and Overhead

Williams College provides a useful example of the degree to which reported expenditures on intercollegiate athletics at schools in *all* divisions, from Division I-A through Division III, understate the full costs of supporting these programs. At first blush, Williams appears to provide an extensive athletics program at a modest net cost. Subtracting the minimal amount of revenue generated by athletics ($152,000) from total expenditures ($1,682,000) implies a net recurring cost of just over $1.5 million. Of this, approximately $1.4 million should be attributed to general administration and lower profile sports, though obviously a good part of the administrative energies of the department may be devoted to football, basketball, and hockey.

Digging deeper reveals a different picture. The "global accounting" concepts developed by Gordon Winston, a professor of economics and former provost at Williams, lead, first of all, to the allocation of roughly $420,000 of central institutional costs (a share of the president's salary, a share of admissions office expenses, and so on) to intercollegiate athletics. This adjustment raises net costs for the whole department to roughly $2 million, and the total for lower profile sports to perhaps $1.6 million.[6] It is capital costs, however, that change the picture dramatically. Professor Winston and his colleagues at Williams have estimated the replacement costs of athletic facilities at Williams (on a building-by-building basis) to be $46.5 million; to this sum, they add the estimated value of related land and athletics equipment ($3.2 million) to obtain a total capital cost of roughly $50 million. They then assume that half of this cost should be assigned to intercollegiate athletics and half to physical education, intramurals, and the like. The final step in the analysis is to assume a depreciation rate of 2.5 percent per year and an opportunity cost of capital of 8.5 percent per year—all very conservative assumptions. The final result is an estimated capital cost for intercollegiate athletics alone of about $2.7 million per year (and approximately $1.8 million for lower profile sports). *The true cost of intercollegiate athletics at Williams, then, is on the order of $4.7 million per year, not the $1.5 million of more easily measured direct costs. Of this more accurate total, $3.4 million can be attributed to the lower profile sports.* These costs supported over 700 intercollegiate athletes at Williams; even so, the true cost per athlete was over $6,500 a year.[7]

Net Operating Costs in Perspective

One way of gaining some perspective is by expressing the current net costs of intercollegiate athletics on a per-athlete basis. As we saw earlier in the chapter, some athletic programs serve the interests of far more students than do others. Dividing total expenditures on athletics by the number of participants makes little sense because of the need to take account of revenue generated by sports such as football and basketball. It is instructive, however, to divide the *net* costs of intercollegiate athletics (subtracting revenue from expenditures) by the number of intercollegiate athletes who, as participants, are the most direct beneficiaries of these general funds outlays. The results of a very crude exercise of this kind (which ignores both capital costs and unallocated central administrative costs) are shown in the white bars in Figure 4.2.

The zero that we have entered for the Division I-A Plus schools reflects the assumption that a very small number of the most elite programs succeed in covering at least the direct costs of all intercollegiate programs out of athletically derived revenues (an assumption that certainly does not hold in all of these situations). The other sets of schools in our study are alike in that none of them can make this claim, but they differ in all other respects. Whereas the overall net costs of intercollegiate athletics may be roughly the same in the Division I-A Standard schools and in the Ivies, the average number of athletes is almost twice as large in the Ivies (850 versus 422); thus the net cost *per athlete* is just over $9,000 in the Ivies but nearly $18,000 in the Division I-A Standard programs included

Figure 4.2.   Net Athletics Operating Expenditure per Athlete Versus Student Services Expenditure per Students (in thousands)

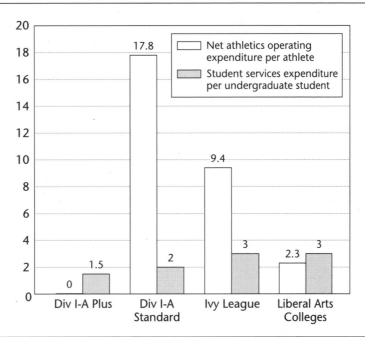

Source: Equity in Athletics Disclosure Act data 1997–98 and Integrated Postsecondary Education Data System 1997–98.

in our study. Duke is a clear exception to this pattern because it has both somewhat lower net costs and appreciably more intercollegiate athletes than the other Division I-A Standard programs; as a result, the estimated net cost per athlete at Duke of $8,500 is very similar to the net cost per athlete in the Ivies. The more favorable financial picture at Duke reflects its success in holding down the costs of football and the fact that its men's basketball program does so well competitively. In short, the high cost of being a Division I-A school can be moderated somewhat by targeting one's aspirations on basketball and being a consistent winner—which it is certainly not easy to do! It is noteworthy that both sets of the Division III schools in our study are estimated to have net costs of roughly $2,500 per athlete— or *less than one-third* of the estimated costs in the Ivy League. Moving up the ladder, from Division III to Division I-AA (the Ivies) to Division I-A, is obviously a very expensive proposition.

One way of confirming that this pattern represents a distinctly athletics phenomenon, tied directly to the levels at which schools choose to compete in sports, is by examining differences across National Collegiate Athletic Association (NCAA) divisions in some other category of expenditures. For this purpose, we have chosen expenditures per student on all student services. These costs turn out to be remarkably similar across divisions, ranging from a low of $1,500 in the large Division I-A Plus schools, to $2,000 in the Division I-A Standard schools, to roughly $3,000 in the Ivies and the Division III schools.[8] When we now compare the net expenditures on athletics per participant (the white bars in Figure 4.2) with the more or less comparable expenditures on student services per student (the shaded bars in Figure 4.2), we see that the two kinds of costs are roughly comparable at the Division III liberal arts colleges; the athletics costs per participant are three times higher in the Ivies and nearly nine times higher at the Division I-A Standard schools; and only in the case of the small number of Division I-A Plus schools are the net operating costs of athletics per athlete estimated to be lower than the student services costs per student.

These comparisons neglect all capital costs of both athletics and student services, and they also ignore the fact that students who are athletes also benefit from general student services. To obtain an additional set of reference points, we asked some schools to provide data on the costs of club sports, intramural programs, and other types of student activities. The scattered bits of information available show a surprisingly consistent picture. Expenditures on club sports and intramurals (added together) ranged from $160,000 at one Division III college to $260,000 at several Division I-A universities that were able to provide data. Outlays for orchestras and other student groups proved impossible to sort out with any precision, but we were able to obtain a list of such activities at one Ivy university that together cost $322,000. For this amount, the university supported bands, an orchestra, dramatic and debate organizations, student government, ethnic organizations, and everything from the Anti-Gravity Society to the Chinese Calligraphy Association. These data confirm the simple but important point that intercollegiate competition entails an entirely different level of financial commitment than the less formal club and intramural sports or the full range of extracurricular activities.

Competition on Other Fronts: SATs of Lower Profile Athletes

The new facilities and shrewder coaches are only going to win if the schools find and admit talented athletes. The increase in recruiting of athletes, documented more fully in *The Game of Life*, reminds us that, as one basketball coach put it, "You can't teach tall; you can't teach fast." Seeking out and admitting talented athletes represents the most substantial, but also the most subtle, battleground for sports competition. At selective colleges and universities, an admissions slot is an extremely scarce resource; at a number of the schools in this study, ten applicants are rejected for every one who is accepted. While there is no hard and fast rule about what the best use of the these scarce admissions places is, and while SAT scores surely are not, on their own, a perfect tool, we can look at trends in test scores to see the degree to which competition for golfers, soccer players, and butterfly specialists has affected the levels of academic preparation that students bring to campus.

One of the most widely circulated myths about college athletes is the image of the "dumb jock," admitted on the basis of his ability to tackle an opposing running back rather than his ability to do mathematics or to hold forth on literature. To test this myth empirically, and to ask whether it has any validity at all in those sports where hardly anyone is watching, we must be much more specific. Is the myth of the underprepared athlete truer at some levels of competition than at others? Have the Ivies and the Division III liberal arts colleges escaped the perceived problems of the universities with big-time athletic programs? Is the myth truer among recent cohorts than it was in earlier eras? And, finally, are there marked differences in the academic credentials of those who play different types of sports?

1989 Cohort Comparisons

We start out by comparing the SAT scores of those athletes in the 1989 entering cohorts, who went on to play both the high-profile sports (football, basketball, and hockey) and the lower profile sports, with the SAT scores of their classmates (students at large). The general pattern is the same in all four sets of schools depicted in Figure 4.3.

The gaps in average SAT scores between students at large and high-profile athletes are large in every set of schools, especially at schools that operate big-time programs. The largest gap in scores (284 points) is at the Division I-A private universities, and this is hardly surprising. These schools recruit athletes who can play football and basketball at the most demanding level of play while simultaneously attracting some of the most academically well-prepared students in the country.

We also find that those playing the lower profile sports also had lower average SAT scores than students at large (with the gaps ranging from roughly 100 to 120 points at the Division I-A level and from 25 to 40 points in the Division III colleges and Ivy League schools).

The Growth in the Test Score Gap

How new are these patterns? We have reliable data for the 1951 cohort for only the Ivy League and the Division III colleges. Even in that early year and in these schools with less intensive athletic programs, lower profile athletes had lower SAT

Figure 4.3.   Average SAT Scores of Entering Male Cohort of 1989

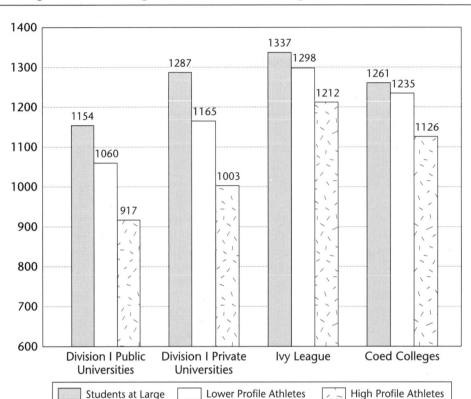

scores than did students at large. So the existence of differences in academic preparation between athletes and other students is not a new phenomenon. It was
also present in the mid-1950s, but the differences were much smaller then. The
gaps in SAT scores among Ivy League lower profile athletes have grown over time:
from 20 points in the 1951 cohort to 30 points in the 1976 cohort to 40 points in
the 1989 group. By the time of the 1989 cohort, the situation had changed
markedly (Figures 4.4 to 4.7). Only a small number of lower profile teams fell
inside the 20 to 30 point range: four in the Ivies, four in the liberal arts colleges,
five in the Division I-A privates, and two in the Division I-A publics. The sports
that most frequently record average SAT scores that are more or less comparable
to the general standard for the school are crew, squash, fencing, golf, and swimming.[9] What is most surprising is the size of the test score gap that has emerged
in a sport like tennis: in 1989, tennis had the second-largest gap of *any* sport in the
liberal arts colleges (−143 points, second only to football) and gaps of more than

Figure 4.4. 1989 Ivy League SAT Divergence from Students at Large, by Sport

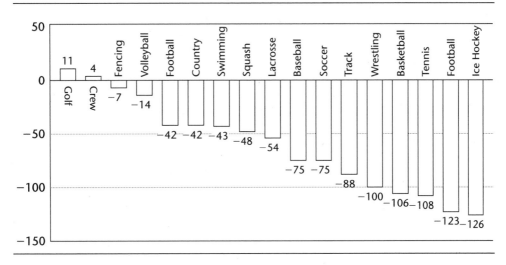

Figure 4.5. 1989 Division III-C SAT Divergence from Students at Large, by Sport

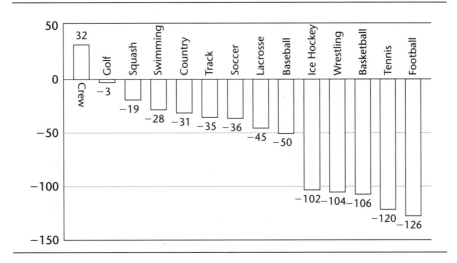

Figure 4.6. 1989 Division I Private SAT Divergence from Students at Large, by Sport

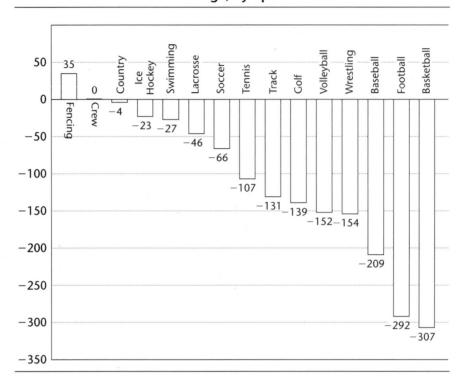

100 points in both the Ivies and the Division I-A private universities. None of these gaps is of course nearly as large as those characteristic of basketball and football (which are in the −300-point range in the Division I-A private universities), but the gaps in these lower profile sports certainly appear to be moving in the same general direction.[10]

In Figure 4.8, we see that women's sports have followed the same pattern as men's, with gaps in SATs widening dramatically between 1976 and 1989 as schools sought to build women's sports up to the level of the men's programs. This sort of "catching up" is clearly another arena in which competition is "succeeding."

At selective colleges and universities, questions of academic preparation have little to do with having enough brainpower to "survive" college. The mean SAT scores of male athletes at the Division III liberal arts colleges and Ivy universities in the study were above the eightieth percentile of all male test-takers nationally; the mean scores of athletes at the Division I-A private and public universities were above the seventieth percentile and the fiftieth percentile,

Figure 4.7.   1989 Division I Public SAT Divergence from Students at Large, by Sport

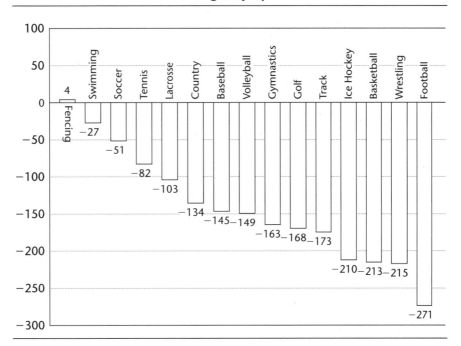

respectively.[11] The athletes at these selective schools are clearly smart people. Nonetheless, there are differences in precollegiate academic preparation between athletes and their classmates, and these differences have generally become much more pronounced over time. These patterns of difference in academic preparation are clear *at every level of play and in many sports—not simply in the high-profile programs at the Division I-A schools.* Women's athletics programs more and more resemble the men's, the lower profile sports look more and more like the high-profile sports, and athletic programs at the nonscholarship schools have taken on more and more of the attributes of the Division I programs.

Competition Without End: Where To from Here?

Seeking anything but the top of the sports rankings may seem like surrender. Resisting these pressures is made even more difficult by the frequent failure to distinguish between *levels of play* (which depend on how talented the athletes are, how much time and how many resources are devoted to preparing for a contest, and

Figure 4.8.   SAT Score Deficit of Female Athletes Versus Students at Large

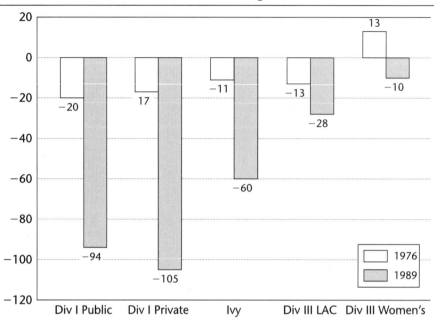

so on) and *vigorous competition* (which can occur, or fail to occur, at any level of play). A competitive cluster of like-minded schools gets the competitive juices flowing for a campus or community whatever the level of play—from Hamilton College field hockey to Penn State football. Heroes in uniforms help to build identity, and they help campus and alumni constituencies to coalesce under a common banner. That is clear. What is more difficult to understand is why it is so hard to convince people that, within the closed ecosystem of the conference, healthy competition does not depend on how expert the play is. A Denison-Kenyon swim meet from 1955 presumably inspired passion even though the times were seconds (or even dozens of seconds) slower than they are today.

Healthy competition requires a rough parity that makes the game worth playing, and sustaining such competition is anything but easy. Even among seemingly like institutions, differences that from a distance would be difficult to detect provide profound competitive advantages (or disadvantages). Within the Ivy League, student bodies of different sizes mean that it is much easier to absorb a few more athletes with lower qualifications in a relatively large school than in a smaller peer. Professional teams recognize that such persistent advantages are detrimental to all and employ revenue sharing, salary caps, and draft pick systems to redress imbalances systemically.

Since the college equivalents of these measures (NCAA regulations and conference rules) never really end the race, an individual school will inevitably continue to act in ways that may make it 5 percent better off, although the whole system may end up 10 percent worse off. Building a new artificial turf field may help your team recruit, but only until the other schools in your league catch up. Then everyone has paid for a new field and its subsequent maintenance, but no one is any better off competitively. The classic example of this sort of behavior occurs when someone viewing a parade stands on his tiptoes to get a better view. Within moments the entire crowd will be on tiptoes, and no one will see any better. No one wants to miss the parade, and the competitive dynamic in sports has unquestionably fueled the increases in expenditures on coaching and facilities at all levels of play. It has also put tremendous pressure on the admissions process. With the unimpeded flow of more and more information about the precollege achievements of athletes, and with the mobility of coaches between institutions, there seems to be no limit to the contagion of athletic expectations. In the end, this dynamic fails all involved. Schools are keenly aware that collaboration in the use of library materials, or even in the sharing of faculty, serves all involved; collaboration in an arena where the essence of the experience is head-to-head competition will never be that sensible. But can there be ways for schools to learn to "play nicely in the sandbox" and escape at least some aspect of mutually assured degradation?

The first lesson is that *as long as individual teams or entire programs are seen as no-cost goods, situations will inevitably worsen.* Awareness that every admissions or budgetary decision has trade-offs must exist at every level. Sometimes understanding these trade-offs is difficult, since evidence is always difficult to compile and difficult to sort through. But efforts must be made to do so.

Beyond this, the system—held together only by the NCAA—must develop ways of acting out of a sense of sector well-being. This, it seems to us, must start with a clear understanding of the facts combined with a clear sense of the missions of the sector and the individual institutions within it. As nonprofits, colleges and universities sometimes seem to be protected from the competitive forces (and tests) that determine the winners and losers in the free market of the for-profit world. The fences around this protected realm have, for a number of reasons, been permeated, leaving schools in between worlds. In some ways, they are competitive with the for-profit world but not in others. Moreover, within this protected realm, institutions (as we have seen) are competitive with each other in some ways that probably do not make a whole lot of sense—when doing so produces no particularly positive end. In the for-profit world, competition leads eventually to better products at better prices, by driving out the inefficient firms or ineffective products. Within higher education, endless raising of the stakes—in the talent of athletes, expertise of coaches, or splendor of facilities—does not seem to achieve any optimal goal. Recognizing the spiraling of the process and quantifying, where possible, the costs of endless competition may be the first steps in convincing the society at large that sometimes the grass may be greener on the other side—only when it isn't.

Endnotes

1. These data sources are described in more detail in *The Game of Life*.
2. More detail about this taxonomy is available in *The Game of Life*.
3. The data in this chapter that are not related to students in the College and Beyond database are taken from the forms prepared by individual schools to comply with the requirements of the Equity in Athletics Disclosure Act (EADA) of 1994. These forms are publicly available and were obtained from the individual colleges and universities.

   All coeducational institutions of higher education that receive federal funding for student aid or any other purpose, and that have intercollegiate athletic programs, must document participation by gender and also provide data that indicate the division of coaching complements, expenditures, and targeted revenues between men's and women's teams. In this chapter, our interest is in the overall dimensions of athletic programs. Women's colleges are exempt from these reporting requirements, and so they are not included in this analysis. There are manifold differences in ways of accounting for athletic expenditures (especially in the treatment of overhead costs and costs of maintaining facilities), and it would be a serious mistake to assume that anything like strict comparability exists across institutions. There are also major problems involved in interpreting data such as average salaries per full-time equivalent coach or staff member, because they do not take account of variables such as length of service. Moreover, all of the reported figures suffer from a failure to make adequate allowance for capital costs, a subject to which we return later in the chapter. Generic problems and anomalies notwithstanding, these EADA data are by far the best available source of information about the finances of intercollegiate athletic programs. As we hope to demonstrate, careful use of the FY 1997–98 reports can provide instructive profiles of patterns of expenditures. We expect that these annual reports will prove even more useful over time as improvements continue to be made in the forms and the accompanying instructions.
4. The figures for the Division I-A schools are taken directly from Table 10 of the EADA reports; the actual average of the figures for the eight Division I-A schools on which this study concentrates is $1,067,000, with a large "clumping" in the $800,000 to $900,000 range. No one should treat the school-by-school differences as precise, since much judgment inevitably entered into the process of presenting these data. The figures for the Ivies and the Division III schools are our own estimates, based on detailed data supplied by five individual schools.
5. More surprising than the differences between the Ivies and the Division III schools are the differences between the Ivies and Division I-A in expenditures per lower profile athlete. These differences reflect the following factors: (1) much larger expenditures on women's basketball in Division I-A; (2) the presence of athletic scholarships at the Division I-A schools; (3) some (but only modest) differences in coaching costs; (4) some differences in

operating and other expenses that reflect, in part, the easier time that the Ivies have in scheduling contests with neighboring schools that have similar programs; (5) a "mix" effect, in that the additional teams that the Ivies field tend to be in relatively less expensive sports such as squash (the "mix" effect also explains why the average expenditure at the Division I-A Plus universities is lower than the average for the Division I-A Standard schools, which support fewer of the relatively inexpensive sports and devote relatively more money to women's basketball); and (6) the presence at the Ivies of more "self-funded" teams, such as wrestling, volleyball, and water polo at Princeton.

6. For the sake of simplicity, we estimate that 67 percent of the administrative and capital costs should be attributed to the lower profile sports. Considering that efforts to recruit and oversee these programs are driven by the numbers of athletes and teams, and also that some of these sports (such as swimming) are extremely capital intensive, these rough estimates seem reasonable.

7. We are indebted to Richard S. Myers, assistant provost and director of Institutional Research at Williams, for this painstaking analysis and to Winston and his colleagues for the underlying analytical framework. For the latter, see Winston and Lewis (1996). There is one other respect in which even this set of numbers underestimates the economic cost of intercollegiate athletics at Williams. Almost all of the Williams coaches also teach physical education, which holds down the costs of intercollegiate sports but almost surely increases the costs of physical education since, in the absence of a strong intercollegiate program, Williams could no doubt hire physical education staff at less than the prorated costs of head coaches of intercollegiate teams.

8. The data showing expenditures on student services are taken from the Department of Education's Integrated Postsecondary Education Data System (IPEDS) forms. The IPEDS glossary defines student services as follows: "Funds expended for admissions, registrar activities, and activities whose primary purpose is to contribute to students' emotional and physical well-being and to their intellectual, cultural, and social development outside the context of the formal instructional program. Examples are career guidance, counseling, financial aid administration, and student health services (except when operated as a self-supporting auxiliary enterprise)." Although no mention is made of intramural and recreational athletics, we know that some schools include this class of expenditures under this heading, and some of the Division III schools, at least, also include the expenses of intercollegiate teams. It is evident from the data, however, that the costs of big-time sports programs are not included here. It is also clear that the treatment of health expenditures varies markedly from school to school, and in arriving at crude averages for divisions we have excluded what appear to be clear outliers.

   It is also possible, of course, to express the net costs of intercollegiate athletics per student, on the theory that all students may be presumed to benefit to some degree from the presence of the intercollegiate athletics program. But the trouble with this approach is that surely it is the tennis players who benefit primarily from the existence of an intercollegiate tennis program, just as it is the students who take classics who benefit mainly (although not exclusively) from the existence of a classics department.

9. Crew has been called "the last of the amateur sports." The relative lack of recruitment of rowers is reflected in their higher average SAT scores.

10. The growing differences between athletes and other students in SAT scores are also reflected in self-reported differences in intellectual self-confidence, in self-ratings of mathematical and writing ability, and in their perceptions of whether they will graduate with honors or

attain at least a B average (as expressed on the Cooperative Institutional Research Program [CIRP] surveys).

11. These comparisons are based on the distribution of verbal SATs among all male college-bound seniors in the 1989 cohort. The results are very much the same if the math SAT is used. National SAT data were obtained from the College Board.

References

Schelling, T. C. *Micromotives and Macrobehavior.* New York: Norton, 1978, pp. 128–129.

Shulman, J. L. and Bowen, W. G. *The Game of Life: College Sports and Educational Values.* Princeton, N.J.: Princeton University Press, 2001.

Winston, G. C. and Lewis, E. G. "Physical Capital and Capital Service Costs in U.S. Colleges and Universities: 1993," February 1996. Available at http://www.williams.edu/Mellon/publications/html.

CHAPTER FIVE

TUITION RISING: WHY COLLEGE COSTS SO MUCH

Ronald G. Ehrenberg

Ehrenberg explores factors that put upward pressure on tuition, including intense competition among institutions to be the very best they can be in every aspect of their activities. Organizational structures, too, add to the pressure: Ehrenberg's research indicates that the "tub model" is widely practiced de facto, reducing central administrations' control over resources. He recommends several steps institutions can consider to help hold down costs, and he urges colleges and universities to assume the mind-set of growing by substitution, not expansion.

Over thirty years ago William Bowen (1967) studied data from a set of selective private institutions and concluded that since the turn of the century their tuition levels had been rising annually, on average, by 2 to 3 percent more than the rate of inflation. He attributed this partially to the increased specialization of knowledge and the growth of new fields of study. But first and foremost, this occurred because the nature of the educational process did not permit academia to share in the productivity gains that were leading to the growth of earnings in the rest of society.

Put simply, the number of students the average faculty member educated each year at these institutions had not changed because low student to faculty ratios were thought to be essential to high quality education. Hence to avoid a decline in the relative earnings of faculty, which might make it difficult to retain existing faculty and attract new ones, tuition had to be increased by more than inflation to provide revenue for salary increases. Inasmuch as real incomes of families were increasing during the period, due to real wage growth and increased female labor force participation, tuition had not risen relative to median family income during most of the period.

In recent years, tuition has continued to increase by more than inflation. However, during the 1980s real income growth in the United States stagnated. As a result, tuition's growing by more than inflation meant that tuition as a share of family income was increasing. Figure 5.1 illustrates this point for Cornell University, but the story is the same for the average selective private institution in the nation. Between 1966–67 and 1979–80 tuition remained roughly 26 to 28 percent of median family income. By 1992–93 this ratio had risen to 49 percent. During the mid-1990s, median family income began to grow again in real terms, and the ratio stabilized at this now higher level. However, the damage had been done. The concern that college costs were taking a greater share of the typical family's income was magnified by the rapid increase in endowments that took place during the booming stock market of the 1990s. Families wondered why the selective institutions even had to raise tuition at all?

I will claim in this chapter that there are a number of forces, in addition to the ones that Bowen discussed, that continue to put upward pressure on tuition. These include the aspirations of academic institutions; our "winner-take-all" society; the shared system of governance that exists in academic institutions; recent federal government policies; the role of external actors such as alumni, local government, the environmental movement, and historic preservationists; periodicals that rank academic institutions; and how universities are organized for budgetary purposes and how they select and reward their deans.

After briefly discussing each of these forces, I will present some results from a survey I recently conducted of large research universities to obtain information

FIGURE 5.1.   ENDOWED CORNELL TUITION AND FEES AS A SHARE OF MEDIAN FAMILY INCOME IN THE UNITED STATES

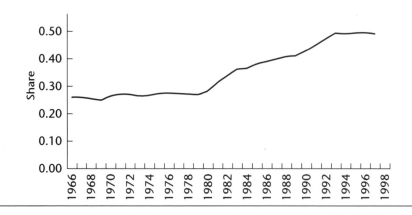

on how they organize themselves for budgetary purposes. Finally, I will conclude with some thoughts on the steps that academic institutions themselves must take if they want to hold down their costs.

Selective Academic Institutions Are Similar to Cookie Monsters

The objective of selective academic institutions is to be the very best that they can in every aspect of their activities. They are like cookie monsters. They aggressively seek out all the resources that they can find and put them to use funding things that they think will make them better. They want better facilities, better faculty, improved research support, improved instructional technology, and better students.

All of these things require more money. While they could aggressively try to increase their efficiency, reduce costs, and get better by substitution rather than growing expenditures, they don't do this for a number of reasons that I will discuss. Rather they adopt the attitude that as long as high quality applicants are flocking to their doors and accepting their offers of admissions, there is no reason for them to moderate their tuition increases.

The "Winner-Take-All" Society

And flock to our doors they do. As Bob Frank and Phil Cook (1995) and Carolyn Hoxby (1997) have pointed out, the fraction of our nation's top students, as measured by test scores, that choose to enroll in the selective private institutions has increased substantially over time. Certainly the development of need-blind admissions and need-based financial aid played a role, as did reductions in transportation and communication costs, in causing this increased concentration of top students.

More recently the increased income inequality in the United States has caused students and their families to increasingly want to (in Bob Frank's terms) "buy the best." My own research with Dominick Brewer and Eric Eide suggests that they are wise to do so, because the economic return to attending a selective private institution rather than another academic institution is large and there is evidence that it has increased in recent years (Brewer, Eide, and Ehrenberg, 1999; Eide, Brewer, and Ehrenberg, 1998).

Each of the selective institutions wants to remain in the subset of schools that students find attractive. So each winds up in what many have called an "arms race of spending" to make itself look better than its competitors. This spending is not restricted to the academic parts of institutions. Institutions also compete with athletics facilities (including fitness centers), new residence halls, and improved dining facilities. For example, Duke has a freshman campus, so Cornell had better have one also.

The quest to be the best is true in graduate education and research as well. It is easier to remain at or near the top in a field than it is to strengthen a weak field and achieve a high level of distinction. As a result, at Cornell we swallow hard as the costs of conducting research in the physical sciences and engineering rise rapidly and continue to heavily devote our resources to these fields in which the university historically has excelled. Pity the poor economist whose models tell him that to minimize costs, one should substitute away from things that have become relatively more expensive (Ehrenberg, 1999a). Pity the poor university that finds that to maintain its historic excellence, it has to skimp in other areas and continue to raise tuition at rates that exceed inflation.

Shared Governance

Why selective private institutions fail to seriously consider the option of reducing their costs, rather than raising tuition, to find the revenue to enhance their operations derives to a large extent from how they are governed. Their system of shared governance between trustees, administrators, and faculty almost guarantees that they will be slow to react to cost pressures.

Trustees are often successful businesspeople who know how to cut costs and meet budget constraints. However, if the president of a university, such as Cornell, tells them that they need to spend money for new initiatives in genomics, advanced materials, and information sciences to maintain the strength of the university and keep it at the forefront of science and engineering, they are likely to swallow hard and go along with him. If the president similarly says that they need funds to enhance the living and learning environment at the university to attract students, they also will likely agree.

There is, however, an important distinction between trustees of private and public universities. Some background data will help to make this clear. In 1978–79, the average full professor at a public doctorate-granting university earned about 91 percent of what his or her counterpart at private doctorate-granting universities earned. This ratio fell steadily during the 1980s and early 1990s until it stabilized at about 78 to 80 percent. This fall in public universities' relative salaries made it difficult for the publics to hire and retain top faculty and invariably led to some decline in these institutions' academic quality.

Similarly, between 1988 and 1994, state appropriations to public higher education per full-time student fell in real terms by about 10 percent. While tuition increases made up for part of this decline, in real terms spending per student fell at many state institutions. During the same time period, real expenditures per student were relentlessly increasing at the selective privates. Hence the disparity between the quality of the two types of institutions grew.

Do these data suggest that trustees of public institutions care less about the quality of their institutions than do trustees of private institutions? In most case the answer is no, although there are some states, such as New York, in which some people have serious questions about the trustees' goals. However, unlike private university trustees, public university trustees often do not have final control over the tuition levels that their institutions charge or their state appropriations. The political process often makes these decisions.

In some states, such as in New York, public university trustees do have control over tuition. However, if the governor lets them know that he wants tuition held constant, it would be foolhardy for the trustees not to accede to his wishes. To do so would leave them vulnerable to the risk of losing their positions. They would also face the possibility that the political process might penalize them by reducing their state appropriation by the amount of the increase in revenue that they gained by increasing tuition. So budgets in public institutions have been cut in spite of their trustees' concern.

Faced with tight budgets due to pressures to reduce state income taxes and the need for more funds for health care, welfare, and the criminal justice system, administrators at the publics make hard decisions and take the steps necessary to balance their budgets. They can always blame the cuts that they must make on state government.

In contrast, if administrators at private institutions were to recommend budget cutbacks, all blame would be assigned to them. They would be widely accused by the faculty of not making a strong enough case to the trustees of the need for higher tuition to maintain institutional quality. Rather than risk losing the support of the faculty, the typical president and provost will often swallow hard and recommend raising tuition by more than they otherwise would prefer to provide some budget relief. After all, administrative terms are not that long, and once an administrator loses the support of the faculty, in most cases it is difficult to effectively lead the institution.

Why is the support of the faculty so important? Under the system of shared governance in place at these institutions, the faculty rules supreme on academic matters. The faculty also feels that it should play a major role in all other decisions at the university. To achieve faculty support for projects is often expensive both in terms of time and dollars. At Cornell for example, the estimated cost of a major new advanced materials research facility has risen from $40 million to $55 million because of modifications that needed to be made to win faculty support for the siting of the building. These modifications, atria to improve the college's environment and improved classrooms, had nothing to do with the underlying academic program for which the building was being constructed.

Federal Government Policies

In recent years the federal government has contributed to the cost pressure on selective private institutions in at least three ways. First, the consent decree between the Ivy League institutions and the Justice Department in the early 1990s now prevents these institutions from meeting to discuss the financial need of commonly accepted individual applicants before financial aid offers are made. While these institutions can, and have, agreed to base financial aid only on financial need, each is now free to determine "need" as it sees fit. This has led to increased use of the practice that has become known as "dialing for dollars" at many Ivy League schools and the other selective privates, as accepted applicants submit financial aid offers from other institutions in an attempt to improve their packages. Put simply it is likely that the consent decree has led to enhanced financial competition for students and improved financial aid packages.

Money for enhanced financial aid programs comes from increased annual giving, increased payout from endowments, increased endowments for financial aid, and increased tuition. The richest institutions may be able to finance their improved programs out of an increased payout from their endowments. However, for most selective private institutions, increased financial aid has required at least some additional recycled tuition revenue. In the absence of the ability to easily cut expenses elsewhere in the budget, the implication is that tuition has had to increase by more than would otherwise be the case.

Second, the value of the maximum Basic Educational Opportunity Grant (BEOG) has not kept up with inflation. Viewed in constant 1997 dollars, the maximum actual BEOG grant rose from $1,500 at the program's inception to over $4,000 in 1975. Since that date it has declined considerably. After falling to under $2,500 in the mid-1990s, it rebounded to $2,700 in 1997. This failure of BEOG levels to keep up with inflation, let alone tuition, required the private institutions to dig deeper into their pockets for financial aid funds; increasingly financial aid has become an institutional responsibility, putting more pressure on tuition.

Finally, the cost of doing research has skyrocketed at the selective private universities in recent years as the federal government has put pressure on private research universities to reduce their indirect cost rates. Between fiscal years 1990 and 1997, the mean indirect cost rate at the thirty-nine largest private research universities fell from 62 percent to 56 percent. In addition, federal agencies began to put more pressure on all institutions to provide more matching funds in grant applications. At the same time that direct-cost funding levels were often being reduced for large center grants, matching fund expectations were growing. Indeed Cornell has found numerous times that to win a renewal of a major center grant at the same, or a smaller, level of funding usually requires the institution to ante up more in matching funds. Funds to make up for the loss of indirect costs revenues and the increased matching cost commitments came from the general operating budgets of the institutions, and this too put more pressure on their tuition levels.

External Actors

Alumni are vital to selective institutions in a number of ways. They contribute funds, help to recruit students, provide internship and postgraduate employment opportunities for students, and support the institution politically. They also have strong preferences about what should be valued and, by strongly communicating these preferences and threatening to withhold contributions, they discourage institutions from cutting almost anything. Similarly, they occasionally provide gifts that academic institutions don't really want because they add to, rather than reduce, the institutions' costs. However, a president rarely refuses such gifts.

Academic institutions also face cost pressures from local governments and interest groups, such as environmentalists and historic preservationists. The institutions are always adding new facilities and renovating old ones. To obtain required construction permits from local governments requires complex discussions and negotiations. Ultimately, these may lead to the institutions having to make increased financial payments to local governments to compensate them for our tax-exempt status. A recent story in the *Chronicle of Higher Education* discussed how much Harvard is increasing its payments to the city of Boston to enable it to develop properties that it owns in the city (Pulley, 1999).

Pressure from environmentalists and historic preservationists may slow down academic institutions' projects and increase their costs by much more than similar pressure would increase the costs of for-profit firms undertaking similar projects.

Unlike business firms, most academic institutions do not have the option of packing up and moving to a new location. Also since they are either public bodies or nonprofits that receive favorable treatment under tax laws, they are expected to make decisions that are in the public interest. For example, Cornell's plans to build a new incinerator to dispose of toxic wastes from veterinary medicine research have been held delayed over four years as the institution tries to assuage environmentalists' concerns. Similarly, Yale recently announced that it was abandoning its plans to demolish several antiquated buildings that comprised its divinity school because it believed that the cost (in time and money) of fighting the battle in the courts would prove prohibitive.

Published Rankings of Academic Institutions

No matter how much institutions criticize published rankings of academic institutions, such as those conducted by *U.S. News & World Report,* they have reason to fear that the rankings may influence students' behavior. A recent study that I conducted with James Monks shows that this fear is justified (Monks and Ehrenberg, 1999).

Using data from thirty selective private colleges and universities over an eleven-year period, Monks and I found that changes in an institution's ranking do influence its admissions outcomes and its financial aid bill. When an institution's ranking improves, this leads to an increase in applicants, a reduction in the fraction of applicants that the institution accepts, an increase in its yield on accepted applicants, an increase in its freshman class's test scores, and a decrease in the amount of financial aid that it must offer to enroll the class.

As a result, institutions have an incentive to take actions that will positively influence their ranking. To the extent that the rankings are partially based on how much an institution spends educating each student, administrators in their right minds would not take actions to reduce the institution's educational expenditures unless they were forced to do so by the trustees. You can imagine how members of the Cornell trustees' finance committee reacted when I told them once (when they were pressing us to behave more like a business and reduce costs) that for us to take action to unilaterally reduce our costs would result in a worsening in Cornell's position in the *USNWR* rankings.

Cornell's rank rose from fourteenth among national universities in the fall 1997 *USNWR* ranking to sixth in the fall 1998 ranking. Not surprisingly there was an increase in applicants for its fall 1999 freshman class, it admitted a smaller fraction of these applicants, its yield rose, and its entering class's test scores rose. Sadly for Cornell, its rank fell back to eleventh in the fall of 1999, primarily because *USNWR* changed the formula that it used to compute the rankings. It was my sad task to inform our president and provost that while I was happy that they were basking in the glory of how well the Cornell freshman class looked this year, our research suggested that Cornell would be lucky if it did as well next year.

How Universities Organize Themselves

The final factors that influence universities' inability to hold down their costs is how the institutions are organized for budgetary purposes and how they select and reward their deans. In Ehrenberg (1999a, 1999b), I discuss these issues in detail. I summarize some of the key points below and present some new evidence on how universities actually are organized for budgetary purposes.

During the spring and summer of 1999 I conducted a survey of the resource allocation methodologies that are used at research and doctorate universities. Over 200 of the approximately 220 institutions in the sample responded to the survey. While I would like to believe that they did so because they recognized my name, more likely it was because William Bowen, the president of the Andrew W. Mellon Foundation, provided me with a cover letter to encourage their participation.

Simplifying greatly, there are four broad types of research allocation methodologies or systems of budgetary arrangements that universities use:

1. *Central control.* Under such a system, all revenue, with the possible exception of some external gifts and the direct costs on external research grants, flows directly to the central administration. The central administration covers its central costs and then allocates some portion of the remaining revenues back to the individual colleges.
2. *Tubs.* Each college is treated as a "tub" on its own bottom. It keeps all of its tuition and other sources of revenue that it generates. It remits funds to the central administration only to cover its allocated share of the central costs. Each college is responsible for all the direct and indirect costs that it incurs, including facilities, maintenance, and operating costs.
3. *Tubs with a franchise fee.* Each college is treated as a tub on its own bottom, but it remits more than its allocated share of central costs to the central administration. The extra amount that the college remits is based on its revenues or its expenditures. This "franchise fee" is then allocated back to the various colleges at the discretion of the central administration or through some priority setting process.

4. *Activity driven.* Under this type of approach, each college remits to the center a share of its total expenditures. The share it remits may differ depending on whether the expenditures are for teaching, sponsored research, or other programs (for example, executive education). No explicit allocation of central costs to different units is made. The center uses the money it receives to cover central costs and then reallocates any excess funds back to the colleges as in the third methodology.

The benefits that a pure responsibility center management (RCM) type model (model 2 above) provides, including the incentives that are present for the units to manage their own resources prudently and to generate revenues, are well known. However, in Ehrenberg (1999a, 1999b), and much more extensively in Ehrenberg (2000), I argue that an unwanted side effect of the approach is that it reduces the incentive for individual colleges to collaborate and to take actions that are in the best interests of the institution as a whole. Put another way, what makes economic sense for a unit does not necessarily help to reduce duplication and hold costs down for the university as a whole.

The first thing that I wanted to know in my survey is how many institutions utilize "pure" RCM models. I asked respondents to ignore the medical colleges in their responses (for reasons that those institutions with medical colleges surely understand). The survey responses indicate that central control is by far the most prevalent form of organization, with 63 percent of the privates and 92 percent of the publics being organized this way. Only twenty-two of the universities were organized as tubs, and this form of organization was most prevalent in private Research I institutions.

Of course how universities are formally organized is not necessarily a good indication of how they actually behave. One provost whom I visited at a best unnamed major public Research I university told me that while all tuition revenue came directly to his office, not the colleges, he had never thought about doing anything other than giving each unit back the tuition revenue that it generated. A second provost whom I spoke to at a public Research II institution told me that while he had the authority to reallocate tuition revenues across the colleges, it caused him too much aggravation to do so.

To see if these attitudes were more widespread, the survey also asked those universities that had answered that the center fully controlled the allocation of revenues whether in practice their incremental allocations deviated substantially from proportionality. In almost half of these institutions in both the public and private sectors, the answer was no. While this may reflect the central administration's satisfaction with the way things are going at each of these institutions, it also may reflect that their colleges are being treated as de facto tubs.

Asking institutions which budget model best fits them may drastically oversimplify things, and the survey also included a set of questions about specific types of income to probe matters further. For example, answers to the question "Is the allocation of tuition revenue from on-campus degree programs under the control of the central administration of your university?" were similar to the answers about central control. However, revenues from nondegree programs (continuing education or executive education) or degree programs off campus (including distance learning programs) were less likely to be under the control of the central administration.

Who "owns" the endowment and who bears the cost of raising new funds are also important dimensions of institutional control. The individual colleges at one private research university that I visited last year keep all of their tuition revenue. At first glance, this institution appears to be organized as a set of tubs. However, the university as a whole has a large endowment that is "owned" primarily by the central administration. As a result, the provost is able to heavily influence the behavior of the units through his control of the allocation of endowment spending.

The survey responses indicate that it is much more likely in public than in private institutions that at least part of the costs of development activities is borne explicitly by the colleges. It is also more likely that this occurs in Research I rather than other institutions. The percentage of endowment spending that is under the control of the central administration varied widely across institutions. However, on the whole, there appears to be more central control over endowment at the private than at the public institutions.

Appointment and Evaluation of Deans

A final important factor that determines whether an institution can behave in an efficient matter and function as a whole is how deans are appointed and evaluated. At many institutions, committees of faculty conduct a search for a dean and then provide the president or provost with an unranked list of the leading candidates. However, the discussion that accompanies that list makes clear who the first choice candidate really is, and typically that candidate is selected.

Once in office, among the dean's primary responsibilities, especially in the universities that operate as tubs, are fund-raising and external relations (with alumni, constituents of the college, state policymakers). If a dean is successful and retains the support of the faculty, it is difficult for a provost or president to penalize the dean (including in the extreme case removing him or her from the position) for failing to cooperate in university-wide initiatives. Deans thus have very little incentive to cooperate in activities that they do not perceive of as being in the best interest of their colleges.

The limited power of central administrators to influence deans' behavior became clear to me when in recent years the presidents of Columbia and Georgetown tried, respectively, to remove and to not reappoint a dean. In both cases, pressure from alumni and key trustees (including the threat of withholding funds) caused the presidents to publicly rescind their decisions. One wonders if the two presidents had failed to follow perhaps the most important advice that a president can be given: never make a major decision on campus that will eventually rise to the level of the trustees without first obtaining key trustees' support.

What Selective Private Institutions Can Do to Help Control Costs

Selective private colleges and universities have been raising their tuition levels, on average, by 2 to 3 percent more than the rate of inflation for at least a century. To achieve some moderation in the real rate of tuition increases will require actions from federal and state government and the institutions themselves. Many of these are discussed in my book (Ehrenberg, 2000). I conclude by briefly mentioning some of the implications of my discussion for institutional policies.

First, as my discussion of the differences between public and private institutions indicated, the trustees of the latter are key actors in efforts to control costs. If efforts to moderate tuition increases are to come, they must be led by the trustees. Without strong directives from the trustees, it is difficult for presidents and provosts to advocate such policies.

Second, the selective universities should organize themselves for budgetary purposes in a way that gives the central administration some control over resources and some leverage to influence the behavior of college deans. If academic institutions are serious about improving the efficiency of their operations and controlling costs, pure tub models are not the way to go. What is in the best interest of an individual unit is not necessarily in the best interest of the university as a whole. Central control over resources removes many of the incentives that units have to raise revenues and hold down their own costs. Hence, variants of the "tubs with franchise fees" or activity-driven models are the preferred alternatives.

Third, college deans at universities must be held responsible for the well-being of the institution as a whole, not just their individual college. This should be an explicit part of their job responsibilities. Faculty and alumni connected to their colleges should be educated to understand that this is an important part of deans' jobs. Serious performance evaluations of deans need to be held annually to reinforce this point.

Fourth, trustees and key alumni need to be educated so that they too understand that what is best for "their" college is not necessarily what is best for the institution as a whole and that they need to think of the latter. This is a hard sell but something that central administrators can profitably devote time to doing.

Fifth, institutions need to conduct regular serious evaluations of all aspects of their academic and nonacademic activities to decide whether efficiencies can be achieved in any activity or whether it makes sense for the institution to stop doing any activity completely. Put another way, the institutions need to get themselves in the mind-set of growing by substitution, not by expansion. Faculty legitimately gripe at having to participate in mindless program reviews that get filed away and that have no impact, so these evaluations must be substantive. There is a trade-off between accountability and collegiality, and serious program reviews may reduce the latter. However, that is a price that the selective institutions may have to pay for trying to be more accountable and holding down their costs.

Finally, institutions should stress much more heavily the sharing of academic and administrative resources, both across units within a campus and across institutions. The announcement earlier this year that Columbia, Yale, and the New York Public Library are building a single repository to house rarely used books of all three institutions is but the tip of the iceberg of things that can be done. More sharing of academic resources by teaching of specialized courses to students on several campuses simultaneously through the use of distance learning technologies is another example. Institutions will have to think very seriously about how they can expand cooperation with their competitors.

Academic institutions are already cooperating on a number of administrative fronts. For example, many are involved in the joint development of information systems for human resources, student services, libraries, development and alumni relations, sponsored programs, and financials. They now need to take the next step and ask if there are ways to share administrative services across campuses to achieve further economies of scale and cost savings. Is it really necessary, for example, for each institution to have its own purchasing department?

This chapter draws on the author's book, Tuition Rising: Why College Costs So Much *(Harvard University Press, 2000).*

References

Bowen, W. J. *The Economics of the Major Private Research Universities.* Berkeley, Calif.: Carnegie Commission on Higher Education, 1967.

Brewer, D. J., Eide, E. R., and Ehrenberg, R. G., "Does It Pay to Attend an Elite Private College? Cross-Cohort Evidence of the Effects of College Type on Earnings." *Journal of Human Resources,* 1999, *34* (Winter), 104–123.

Ehrenberg, R. G. "Adam Smith Goes to College: An Economist Becomes an Academic Administrator." *Journal of Economic Perspectives,* 1999a, *13* (Winter), 99–116.

Ehrenberg, R. G. "In Pursuit of University-Wide Objectives." *Change,* 1999b, *31* (January/February), 29–31.

Ehrenberg, R. G. *Why Colleges Can't Control Their Costs.* Cambridge, Mass.: Harvard University Press, 2000.

Eide, E. R., Brewer, D. J., and Ehrenberg R. G. "Does It Pay to Attend an Elite Private College? Evidence on the Effects of Undergraduate College Quality on Graduate School Attendance." *Economics of Education Review,* 1998, *17* (October), 371–376.

Frank, R. H. and Cook, P. J. *The Winner-Take-All Society.* New York: Free Press, 1995.

Hoxby, C. H. "The Changing Market Structure of U.S. Higher Education: 1940–1990." Mimeo, Harvard University Department of Economics, 1997.

Monks, J. and Ehrenberg, R. G. "*U.S. News & World Report*'s College Rankings: Why They Do Matter." *Change,* 1999, *31* (November/December), 42–51.

Pulley, J. L. "In Bid to Ease Town-Gown Tensions, Harvard Increases Its Payments to Boston." *Chronicle of Higher Education,* September 10, 1999, p. A54.

PART THREE

PLANNING FOR THE FUTURE

CHAPTER SIX

"WHEN INDUSTRIES CHANGE" REVISITED

New Scenarios for Higher Education

David Collis

Collis describes the potential deconstruction of the traditional university caused by technology and new entrants to the higher education market. The many alternatives for learning that technology presents break down much of the rationale for vertical and horizontal integration of higher education on a traditional campus. At the same time, changing and growing demand provides opportunities for new companies to enter the field by serving emerging markets. Collis offers strategic approaches for colleges and universities to consider in response to their deteriorating industry structure.

In Collis (1999) I argued that the future of higher education was likely to be more competitive than at any time in the past. New entrants would exploit the profit potential of higher education by capitalizing on emerging technologies to "cherry pick" its most desirable segments, such as executive education. Buyers would become increasingly price sensitive, and important groups of them—notably corporations—would backward integrate into the provision of their own services. Faculty, as key suppliers of the intellectual material for higher education, would be able to leverage copyrights on their ideas into "superstar" salaries and ownership stakes in nontraditional media, such as videos, CDs, and the Internet. Finally, rivalry among existing institutions, while mitigated by growth in the student body as the echo of the baby boom passed through higher education, would increase as a technology with high fixed costs but essentially zero marginal costs provided universities an economic incentive to expand and even intrude on each others' geographies.[1]

I suggested that the result of this competition would not only be harder times for institutions of higher education but also the potential unraveling of the traditional vertically integrated, full product range university. In its place one could imagine the university as a smaller, more specialized provider of a limited set of educational programs—probably based around a three-year residential liberal arts degree that socializes students and teaches them how to learn but does not dispense a particular body of knowledge that is expected to satisfy their needs for life.

The passage of a year has only convinced me that my suggestions were too limited and too cautious and that they will occur much faster than I ever believed possible in 1998. A cursory review of recent press coverage of private sector entry into secondary education only reinforces this judgment, with headlines such as "The Business of Universities" (*Boston Globe*), "Wiring the Ivory Tower" (*Business Week*), "A Different Course" (*Wall Street Journal*), and even *Parade* magazine's "Go to School Again." Indeed, Peter Drucker, the management guru, has argued that "Universities won't survive. The future is outside the traditional classroom" (Callahan, 1999).

To convince you that this is the case, and maybe also heighten your paranoia, in this chapter I will first review some of the recent developments and data that suggest the private sector is finally committing resources to its vision for the future of higher education. Then to address concerns that were expressed about the blanket nature of my remarks in Collis (1999), I will outline how four different entrants might approach the industry and suggest how their strategies will differentially affect various tiers among current institutions. As I did in Collis (1999), I will conclude by suggesting some possible responses that universities can (and probably should) take to avoid entering a downward spiral of lost programs and declining enrollment that could force price increases, exacerbate market share loss, and so on.

Private Sector Involvement in Higher Education

You are all aware of Internet stock mania—and I trust that some of you have benefited from it institutionally and personally—but how many of you know of the education stock mania? How many of you know the number of education company stocks that are publicly traded? Or how large the market is for public companies competing in the education sector? In 1999 Merrill Lynch published a 193-page research report, *The Book of Knowledge* (Moe, Bailey, and Lau, 1999), which laid out this data for investors; it is the best indicator of the burgeoning private sector interest in education in general and higher education in particular.

Perhaps the most compelling statistic in the Merrill Lynch report is that the education sector as a whole represents nearly 10 percent of the United States' gross national product (GNP) today and yet receives less than 0.2 percent of private capital formation. Higher education alone, defined as all postsecondary education, represents a market of $237 billion, of which only $5 billion is served by the private sector. Just as nature abhors a vacuum, so competition abhors an unserved market. Indeed, higher education is like health care thirty years ago, poised for takeover by the private sector. In fact, that industry's share of U.S. private sector capital markets has gone from 3 percent in the 1970s to 14 percent today (Stone, 1999). The only deterrent to private sector entry into higher education, apart from philosophical objections to the presence of the profit motive in education, has been the huge sunk cost and unprofitability of the traditional university. As I discussed in Collis (1999), and as I will sketch in the next section, technology and changes in the demand for and timing of higher education now facilitate focused, low-cost, and profitable private sector entry.

Technology

The first of the two drivers facilitating entry by the private sector is technology. Again, I do not want to dwell on the mechanics (though perhaps electronics would be a better word) of the Internet or other technological advances. What I can do is highlight their effects on a couple of dimensions.

There are several ways that companies or universities can employ the new technologies to expand or improve the educational experience. Institutions can use technology to ease the capacity constraint in existing facilities for students that are on campus; expand geographical coverage to parts of the state or the country that it does not already serve; and enter new markets or niches, such as corporate training. They can even transform the current pedagogy used in the classroom—going beyond the use of the Internet as a distributed printer of course material, as a replacement for office hours, or as a camera on the classroom. Beyond this, of course, technology can transform a university's own value chain by fundamentally altering internal administrative functions and processes.

But even before technology goes this far, when the Internet is merely a channel of distribution, it can have a dramatic effect on industries. Those of you that disagree because of the inferiority of the current product ignore historical lessons about the surreptitious effect of technologies that appear at the low end of a market. Many of these technologies were ignored or slighted by incumbents because they were inadequate for the needs of current customers. Yet the technologies were stealthy competitors that crept up on those unwary and complacent players who too quickly dismissed the threat with criticisms of their inferiority and testimonials from buyers trumpeting the merits of the existing technology.

What makes some new technologies so insidious is that they first appear as ineffective substitutes that can safely be disregarded. The best-selling management text by my colleague Clay Christensen makes exactly this point. In countless instances of what Christensen calls "disruptive technologies," from disk drives, to personal computers, and now the Internet, technological advances initially yield products that fail to satisfy current users (Christensen, 1998).[2] The product is too slow, too expensive, too limited, and so on. Incumbents that do the right thing and listen to their customers are told that this is not what customers want. Accordingly, the market leaders ignore the new technology and continue to refine their existing products and technology.

There are two errors in this response, which turns out to be merely rearranging chairs on the Titanic. First, the development trajectory of the new technology may well be faster than for the existing mature technology. In disk drives, for example, although smaller drives were initially slower and had less storage capacity, design limitations on older larger drives had already been reached. In contrast, researchers were just discovering the capabilities of the new technology. Within a couple of years smaller drives became superior.

Even if Internet-based education is inferior to the traditional classroom today, what might it look like in a few years when faculty have had the opportunity to experiment with the technology? Looked at the other way, how much potential is there for advances in traditional pedagogy? Several centuries of experience suggests that we are unlikely to get much better at delivering courses in the classroom than we are today. What might two centuries of development on the Internet, or even two decades (or two years!), do for improvement in delivering courses through that channel of distribution?[3]

The second flaw in a strategy that ignores new technologies because they do not satisfy current users' needs is that there are often different customers or potential customers whose needs are not currently met but for whom the new technology is perfectly adequate. Personal computers were for many years not as effective as minicomputers, and universities could never see how they could replace the DEC Vax 10s in their central computing facilities with the new product. Yet individual faculty and administrators rapidly adopted a technology that satisfied their more limited but otherwise unmet computing needs. Locked into serving its institutional customers with powerful minicomputers, Digital never seriously embraced the PC and now no longer exists (partly because of the first argument—seventeen years after the introduction of the IBM PC we now have in our briefcases a computer that has more power than the old Vax 10 workhorse of many university computer facilities).

In higher education today, four-year undergraduate degree residential students may well protest that distance learning and the Internet are no substitute for the quality of the education they are receiving on campus. But everyone else who cannot afford the expense, the time, or the relocation disturbance of a residential program might well embrace the technology as satisfying their very different, and somewhat less demanding, needs at a very attractive price. Within a few years, new entrants employing the new technology and exploiting its inherent scale economies and innovation trajectory could offer a product that is as good as current degree courses at lower cost. And a few years after that . . .

The Boston Consulting Group (BCG) has identified another important effect that the Internet can have on industries, which they have labeled "deconstruction" (Evans and Wurster, 1997, 2000).[4] They argue that the Internet for the first time transcends the trade-off between reach and richness in the interaction between organizations and individuals. Historically, when companies wanted to communicate with a mass audience they had to provide very limited content in the message—the typical thirty-second television commercial. When, instead, companies needed a rich interaction that conveyed much information and was responsive to the unique needs and concerns of individuals, they had to use a forum with very limited reach—the salesman in a car dealership. The Internet has broken through this frontier by allowing companies to interact with millions of people and yet provide vast amounts of customized information to each one.

BCG goes on to argue that transcending the richness and reach frontier allows small specialist competitors to be efficient in industries that previously required size and scope for profitability. Amazon.com, for example, could not have entered bookselling without the advantage over bricks and mortar bookstores, like Barnes and Noble, of offering 5 million titles to individual consumers. E*Trade has disaggregated the full-service brokerages by offering the complex interaction of stock trading by itself. It is the emergence of such players that leads to the "deconstruction," or vertical and horizontal disintegration, of entire industries.

In higher education the analog would be the deconstruction of the traditional university. At one level the argument is simply that the Internet breaks down the trade-off between richness and reach, providing the richness and customization of content that are required for an effective educational experience for a large number of students at once. That is the threat of distance learning, although this time with the emphasis on the volume of students that can be educated on-line, rather than on their physical dispersion.

At another, deeper level the argument is that the technology facilitates entry by specialist providers because it takes away some of the traditional rationales for vertical and horizontal integration. Students can, for example, now pick and choose courses from many suppliers by searching the Web not just for two-paragraph course descriptions but for the complete set of course materials, including all reading lists, assignments, presentations, handouts, and so on. They can probably even see the lecturer in action on video clips and read a set of student evaluations. In short, the sort of detailed information that was traditionally only available to students on campus can now be part of a student's process for selecting courses among universities, or in deciding to take the one great course provided by a new entrant.

In this environment, the reputation of the institution as a whole is not the only external signal of the quality of its courses. The Internet enables students to be far more discriminating in their assessments. This suggests that brand name becomes a much less powerful deterrent to entry, particularly if entrants can gain instant credibility by utilizing teaching materials from brand name institutions. If Harvard professor Eric Maskin makes available a great course on microeconomics through a new entrant, students will most likely prefer to take that rather than suffering through the poor quality course offered at the state university they are attending.[5]

If the Internet leads to the horizontal unbundling of the university, it can also lead to the vertical deconstruction of universities by eliminating the need for the joint provision of many activities, most obviously residential accommodation, but also the library (books have a very rich content) and even classroom space. Ending the requirement for a credible competitor in higher education to provide an integrated bundle of activities clearly reduces entry barriers enormously.

The arguments above are only two of the more recent and well-received ideas from research in strategy about the likely impact of new technology, notably the Internet,[6] on industries. Even so, they combine to provide a picture that I hope illustrates the very real and current threat posed to higher education today by private sector companies.

Demand

If technology offers the way to supplant traditional entry barriers, changes in demand provide the market opportunity for new entrants. Current projections show there will be about a 20 percent increase in the number of eighteen-year-old students entering higher education by 2010.[7] This echo of the baby boom appears to be a captive market for universities, which can anticipate with glee (if also some concerns about space shortages) their ever-increasing enrollments. But consider for a moment the broader market for higher education, beyond eighteen-year-olds seeking undergraduate degrees.

Today, 43 percent of students in higher education are over twenty-five years old (Moe, Bailey, and Lau, 1999). By 2010 the expectation is that such mature students will be in the majority because of the increasing requirements of the economy for a more educated workforce and the desire of individuals to bridge the widening income gap between college and high school graduates.[8]

Mature degree students require a very different educational experience than eighteen-year-olds. They are already socialized and so do not require the university to act *in loco parentis*. The opportunity cost of their education is high since they have jobs and higher earning potential than teenagers. They are unlikely to relocate for their education since they already have their own homes and are not desperate to escape from living with parents. They only have limited time available to spend on their education since they have full-time jobs and families of their own, and the academic calendar is meaningless to their annual cycle.[9] What these mature students need is a part-time degree program that is easily accessible from their homes at times and dates convenient to them.[10] If the price is low, so much the better.

Universities do not offer such programs, and yet this is a large potential market—75 percent of Americans over twenty-five lack a degree. This unserved market is, therefore, a huge attraction to private sector entrants that can exploit technology to deliver the convenient low-cost product these customers demand. Given this entry path, companies that build scale and a reputation in this segment should be able to move upmarket into a more traditional degree program. Americans laughed at the "Made in Japan" label in the 1960s; bought cheap, small, but fuel efficient cars from that country in the 1970s; yet by the end of the 1980s, recognized Lexus and Infiniti as equal to, if not better than, the best traditional European luxury cars.

Beyond simply offering undergraduate degrees for mature students, there is a powerful drive for extending adult education. As knowledge accumulates at a rate that makes obsolete the set of skills acquired at twenty-one years old by age thirty, the model of postsecondary education will shift from onetime to lifelong learning. This will result in a growth in demand for specific skills training (as well as for the more traditional extension school adult education[11]) and provide another huge opportunity for private sector entrants that is currently internally served by corporate universities and training departments.

As I suggested in Collis (1999), the societal changes that are involved in this shift in demand toward lifelong education are as fundamental as the alteration in the implicit employment contract, from lifetime employment to "free agency." The trend to nontraditional students in higher education will not, therefore, go away. Rather it will accelerate as the variety of product offerings for these market segments expands and as their prices inevitably come down as they exploit the scale economies inherent in new technologies. This shift in the composition of the demand for higher (postsecondary) education, therefore, foreshadows a fundamental change in the very nature of the industry, by inducing new private sector companies to serve the emerging market segments.

Implications

The changing demand for education and the capabilities offered by new technologies facilitate entry into the market by for-profit organizations that pick off an underserved niche with a novel, and profitable, business model. Naturally, this opportunity has not escaped the gaze of the capital markets.

In the postsecondary market it is estimated that of the 3,700 schools providing service, 345 are proprietary (Moe, Bailey, and Lau, 1999). New flows of capital to the sector are also increasing. Since 1994 sixty-eight initial public offerings (IPOs) and other capital market offerings have raised $3.4 billion for education and training companies, partly because the education sector as a whole has returned 134 percent to shareholders over that period, compared to only a 54 percent increase in the Russell 2000 Index. The largest twelve publicly quoted companies in higher education, including Apollo Group (parent of the University of Phoenix), Sylvan Learning, and DeVry, now have a combined market capitalization of $6 billion, while private investors include the Pritzer family (owners of the Hyatt hotel chain), the Carlyle Group, and, of course, Michael Milken and Chris Whittle.

Perhaps the best example of private sector investment is the University of Phoenix. Many of you know that it is now the largest private university in the U.S. with over 60,000 students, but did you know that its parent—the Apollo Group—has also been one of the best stock market performers over the last five years, providing a total return of 1,550 percent to shareholders since IPO in 1994, and with a current market capitalization of about $2 billion (Moe, Bailey, and Lau, 1999)? The company has struggled and experimented with various approaches in the past, but it is now in the process of rolling out a business model that works and is continually extending that model.

To a frequent business traveler, the University of Phoenix is almost ubiquitous. Somewhere, within ten miles of most airports I visit, I see a University of Phoenix building. This is intentional. Phoenix is not a distance learning institution; it is a convenient institution. Facilities are located with adequate parking spaces on major highways and along bus routes and are open at convenient times. Courses are primarily offered after work hours, and courses begin so frequently that all students should be able to start their program within days of signing up. Classes are small—average class size is sixteen—and are taught by part-time faculty, most of whom have full-time jobs. Indeed, only 100 of their 5,200 nonadministrative staff are full-time employees. Prices are set to be somewhat above comparable in-state tuitions.

The result of this strategy is a $0.5 billion enterprise with profit margins of 18 percent. With sixty-five campuses spread over twelve states, Phoenix intends to expand rapidly and to enter true distance (Internet-based) learning. And the University of Phoenix only educates 0.5 percent of all postsecondary students. What a market opportunity!

Many of you may be thinking, so what? What if entrants capture the emerging market segments? Universities have never had the mission or obligation to serve all postsecondary students. A shift in the composition of overall demand will not affect our traditional student body, which is still set to expand over the next fifteen years. The new entrants might well expand the total market for higher education, but they won't affect our traditional student body.

In the short term, of course, this is true. Nothing is going to reduce the enrollment of eighteen-year-olds in undergraduate programs over the next five years or so. But two factors, one of which I have mentioned already, are likely to have an important impact during that time.

The first threat posed by entrants serving new market segments is that of a "disruptive technology." Over time the entrants' new business model, or technology, will offer programs at such attractive prices and feature combinations that they will begin to attract traditional students. Obviously those existing institutions most at threat here are the smaller nonresearch state schools, which today come as close as any college or university to serving such students. Higher-end residential and research universities that offer a liberal arts, tutorial-based education will clearly be the last to face competitive pressures from this source. But as the examples of the U.S. auto industry, the U.K. motorbike industry, the U.S. steel industry, and many other industries illustrate, the period of protection for those at the high end might only be twenty years at the very most and may well be substantially shorter.

For high-end institutions, particularly state rather than private schools, the second and more immediate threat might simply be price pressure. As an example, consider the teaching hospitals, which as premier institutions have been insulated from many of the changes in the health care industry.[12] The one change they have not been able to avoid has been cost comparisons with other hospitals. Today there is enormous pressure on teaching hospitals to reduce their costs and prices because it is publicly and repeatedly pointed out that their cost per bed day is substantially higher than other hospitals. While teaching hospitals protest loudly about differences in the services they provide that justify the higher costs, the fact remains that they are being squeezed by the comparison with other, particularly for-profit, hospitals.

The same could well happen in higher education. Even if entrants do not immediately take away students from the premier universities, the cost pressure imposed by comparisons of student tuition rates will be enormous. If an entrant can provide a degree course at $5,000 per year, for example, how can you justify $20,000 per year (I exclude room and board fees) for the same degree (which might well include some of the same courses taught remotely by the same professors)? State officials and politicians, in particular, will be very conscious of such comparisons because higher education makes up a large percentage of their budgets. And when a university system requests a several-billion-dollar bond issue to fund the renovation of facilities and investment in new technology, will it pass muster in the legislature that observes the proliferation of lower cost educational alternatives?

What will make these cost pressures worse, of course, is that the entrants will be picking off the more attractive parts of higher education. Executive education is one of the few programs that is profitable on a full-cost basis at most institutions, and yet that will be the first to be lost to entrants.[13] Even "unprofitable" programs (which describes most programs) make a contribution to the fixed costs of the university. As a result, any loss in students or programs increases costs for the remaining students, unless the institution is prepared to close down whole departments or schools. This leads to the "deconstruction" of the university that I am suggesting may well happen.

The net effect of the two changes I outlined will, therefore, be pressure on all institutions of higher education. Some will be affected directly, some indirectly, but all will feel the repercussions of a changing industry sooner rather than later.

Four Entry Strategies

To exemplify the threat to universities posed by the private sector, I will describe possible strategies that four new (and old) participants in the industry might pursue. While these are hypothetical and incomplete strategies, they are not unrealistic. Indeed, elements are already being adopted by certain competitors. The four chosen strategies describe a range of positionings that players might pursue, from the high to the low end. Taken together they illustrate how all the various institutions of higher education will be affected by the upcoming change in the industry, even if the specific effects for each will come from a different direction and will impact in different ways.

I have attached names to the institutions pursuing each of the four strategies to personalize the descriptions. They are, however, not intended to be attributed to those companies alone. Rather the strategies are representative of those that could be adopted by any organization of that generic type. I have also presented the strategies as a set of definitive actions, unqualified by adverbs, such as *might* or *could*. Again this does not imply these are the exact strategies that will be pursued; it is merely a more assertive form of presentation.

Harvard University (Research Institution)

I start with an institution that is a current player in higher education. I do this intentionally because the threat to the traditional university comes not only from outside the industry but also from farsighted players that capitalize on the same opportunities seen by outsiders. I do not necessarily put Harvard in this category but choose it as the illustration simply because I know it the best.

As an organization that manages itself according to the aphorism "Every tub on its own bottom," the strategy of the university is unlikely to be coordinated. Rather it will be the sum of the independent strategies of the various schools. Instead of being exhaustive, and somewhat repetitive, in covering all the schools, I will, therefore, focus on two—the undergraduate College and the postgraduate Business School.

As competition for undergraduates intensifies, the appropriate strategy for the premier private universities is to play to their strengths. In the case of Harvard College (and others), these are primarily brand name, physical facilities, financial resources, and the capabilities of the faculty and student body. Harvard will, therefore, leverage those assets by promoting itself as the leading provider of the traditional residential undergraduate degree, based at its Cambridge campus.

The value of the Harvard brand will be reinforced by appropriate marketing (probably focused on public relations campaigns that continually mention Harvard and direct marketing to schools). Some of the endowment will be invested to improve the physical facilities in order to differentiate the quality of Harvard's dormitories, classrooms, and so on from other schools. The size of the undergraduate body is unlikely to expand substantially, although initially Harvard would expand its presence internationally by marketing to foreign students. Later, however, by opening international campuses to allow all students to receive part of their education overseas, capacity could be increased.

All of this, and much more I could describe, may sound obvious and nonthreatening, but potentially the biggest change at the undergraduate level would be the introduction of merit scholarships. Although Harvard might not want to initiate competition on this dimension, the ending of the antitrust exemption for universities encourages someone to break ranks and cut prices selectively (which is the purpose of merit scholarships) to attract the best students.

Unfortunately, the more that higher education becomes a signal of quality, whose greatest benefit is not necessarily the education itself but the association with an institutional brand name, the more important the quality of other students becomes.[14] This arises, first, because the quality of an on-campus residential education comes as much from the interaction with other students as it does from the formal educational process itself. The higher the quality of the other students, the better the education I get. The second reason is that after graduation, the higher the quality of students, the better the peer group network that I have access to in order to further my career.[15] The third reason is simply the reputation effect. If most students from Harvard do well, then it is a good bet that any single student with a degree from Harvard will do well.

The dynamic established by such forces is that the best students want to associate with the best students. Any university that can demonstrate the quality of its student intake through SAT scores and such will, therefore, become more attractive to other good students, which raises the average SAT score and so creates a virtuous circle.[16] In contrast, universities that cannot maintain the quality of the student body in this "winner-take-all" market enter a downward spiral of declining student quality.

The temptation for every institution to offer merit scholarships to attract the best students is, therefore, enormous. Harvard can always ensure that it wins this game, even if it doesn't initiate the competition, by putting some of its endowment to work in merit scholarships. Giving free tuition to the top three students in every state would cost $18 million per year; this represents less than 2 percent of Harvard's budget, a small sum by private sector standards to spend on advertising and marketing.[17]

A similar dynamic operates, of course, at the faculty level. Good faculty are easier to recruit when there are other high quality faculty present. Bidding for Nobel Prize–winning professors has already occurred, and not just on the salary level. Packages now include salary, named chairs, minimal teaching requirements, and large research budgets over which the professor has complete control.

"To those that have, shall be given" is the probable result of these dynamics among the leading universities. The richer institutions will pull away from the poorer institutions and will form their own tier at the apex of higher education. How many institutions will be able to make the transition to this nirvana is unclear. What will certainly increase that number is the willingness of top universities to differentiate themselves, not in quality terms, but in terms of adopting a specialization. If it is known that Harvard and Princeton are best for economics, MIT and Caltech for engineering, Yale and Dartmouth for history, and so on, more institutions will be able to be the best.[18] If all try to be all things to all people, many will fall by the wayside in the competition to capture the "best" all-around students.

The strategy of the Harvard Business School will be more consciously expansive. Partly this is because of the missionary tradition of the school, which has always interpreted its role as benefiting society by raising the standard of management around the world.[19] Partly it is because of the profitability of executive education, and partly because of the competitive need to maintain a dominant global brand name.

This expansion will primarily be international. The school will open satellite campuses in Asia (as INSEAD, the top European business school, already has) and Europe, which will offer short courses to local executives. It will also enter the distance learning market, capitalizing on demand for high quality—and high priced—executive programs that have the convenience and lower cost of local provision.[20]

This will be accompanied by the mass marketing of self-teaching materials, so that the school earns the royalties from those materials, not the faculty nor third-party publishers. Already the school offers written, video, and CD materials that allow the user to study from the gurus of management education, and it is working with a private sector company, Pensare, to expand its offerings. While it is unlikely that the Harvard brand would ever be used for certificates or degrees that were not controlled by the school, the availability of such materials for other institutions or companies to use in their own programs would still pose a threat to other business schools. When a corporate university can offer an in-house Harvard course, why send managers to an expensive course at another business school?

This is the real threat that high quality institutions pose to other universities. The ability to profit from courses which can now, for the first time, be replicated at zero marginal cost allows institutions with brand names to expand their market share and capture additional profits. Already, Harvard, Wharton, Columbia, Stanford, and Chicago business schools are, one way or another, reselling existing courses beyond their campuses.[21] This places pressure on second- and third-tier institutions that lack a brand name or other source of differentiation and reinforces an outcome in line with the aphorism "to those that have, shall be given."

In fact, this might well lead to a real bifurcation of the industry. The top-tier institutions could shift back to the tutorial system to differentiate their on-campus education, while capitalizing on their brand name to make the basic lectures and courses available to third parties via the new technologies. Second-tier institutions, in contrast, will have to embrace the Internet and employ lower-cost teaching methods in order to compete with the new distance learning entrants who use those brand name courses to gain instant credibility.

Note that because there is now an opportunity to resell courses outside the university, Harvard will have to alter its policy towards intellectual copyright so that not only research but also course development will become the property of the university. Owning the copyright to courses will be the only way for the university to retain its share of the profit stream generated by course development, and, more importantly, preserve the value of the Harvard brand by controlling its use.

Open University (Distance Learning)

I choose the Open University as the representative entrant into the distance learning market because it has a track record and credibility. It has also recently announced its entry into the U.S. market.

The Open University has a long and distinguished history in the U.K. Today it has over 100,000 students, of whom the majority are over age twenty-five. While many students take individual courses, several thousand graduate with bachelor degrees each year; indeed the Open University graduates one-quarter of all the MBAs in the U.K. each year.

The expected entry strategy for the Open University into the U.S. will replicate many aspects of its U.K. strategy because it will target the same mature student segment. That strategy has always involved a mix of distance learning technologies—originally television and mail correspondence, but now the Internet and e-mail as well—and some limited time on a campus. The primary educational vehicle in this model, however, has been the interaction with a tutor who is a part-time employee of the university and who is, remotely, responsible for review of the regular assignments that accompany the lectures and classes. The result of this model is that while students ostensibly take lectures in huge classes—one television show is viewed by all students taking the course—the more important tutor-student ratio is, at about 15:1, much lower than a typical university class size.

If this sounds like an inferior product, pause for a moment to consider the investment the Open University makes in pedagogy. Full-time faculty are chosen for, and primarily spend their time, on course development, with some time on supporting tutors but very little time actually teaching. Instead faculty devote themselves to finding the best pedagogical approach to a subject and working with the leading experts in a field to capture the current state of knowledge. Typically a course will cost $1.5 million to develop, with no expense spared if it is deemed educationally necessary. Experts might be flown to South America for filming, computer graphics will be custom programmed, and so on.

I would guess that most of your institutions allocate none of their budgets explicitly to new course development and that none expect research faculty, who have no interest in pedagogy, to develop their own courses. And you still maintain that the Open University product is inferior! How does your institution's university-wide budget on pedagogical developments on the Internet compare to the Open University expenditure of $1.5 million per course?

How can the Open University support such a huge investment in course development? One answer is that the course material is not updated as often as lecturers update their material (though the wrinkled notes we have all seen professors bring to class might suggest otherwise). But the real explanation is that the Open University cost structure is very different. With the bulk of the teaching performed by relatively low-paid part-time tutors who are paid only for teaching, the cost per hour is closer to $50 than the $500 for a research institution.[22] While these numbers are obviously grossly simplified, and make the comparison only with research institutions, the fact is that the cost of paying part-timers just for teaching is much lower than subsidizing the research of full-time faculty.[23] A cost advantage of 90 percent is enormous by private sector standards and obviously will attract entrants who can use the advantage to invest in course development and smaller class sizes (as the Open University does) or take the difference in lower prices and higher profits.

To implement this strategy in the U.S., the Open University is pursuing joint ventures with two-year colleges. Each side can contribute something valuable to the alliance. The Open University will contribute the allure of a reputable undergraduate degree that the colleges can offer.[24] In turn the colleges can provide their facilities—widespread and conveniently located—and their faculty, which is an obvious source for tutors. The result could be a high quality, convenient degree program attractive to many mature students. While this threat is most immediate for institutions currently serving that market, the potential for attracting students from universities should be apparent.

The Open University is a hybrid model of distance learning, mixing tutors and campus time with self-study. A pure model of self-study distance learning is even lower cost, if somewhat lower quality. It is reasonable to anticipate entry into this market will occur by firms pursuing a variety of models, which will only increase pressure on institutions serving this segment of the market.

Harcourt General (Publisher)

Harcourt is representative of a number of textbook publishers that could enter this low end of the higher education market by offering a set of courses that students patch together to complete a degree. It has already announced its commitment to do so, hiring the former Massachusetts education commissioner to run its new Internet University (Hechinger, 1999).

The incentive for publishers to enter the market is that they already have a supply of course materials and relationships with faculty that have demonstrated expertise in effective course development. If they can leverage these assets by forward integrating into the educational parts of the value chain, they will be able to appropriate a much larger share of the higher education dollar—textbooks represent only 1 percent of total expenditure on higher education.

Since publishing on the Internet has much lower fixed and variable costs than traditional book publishing, the cost of experimentation is low, as is the break-even sales level for an individual course. As a result, at every academic conference I attend these days, publishers are voraciously competing to put our courses on-line.[25] This offer of on-line publishing includes presentation slides, assignments, and all teaching materials, as well as hyperlinks to relevant literature and other Web sites. Authors are happy to find a profitable outlet for their courses, from which they would otherwise be unable to capture any value, and publishers extend their course catalogue at relatively low cost.

While the current model of on-line publishing supports traditional institutions by providing turnkey courses that still require some element of faculty delivery, it could easily be amended to be more directly competitive.[26] Adding staff to grade assignments would begin to replicate the Open University model, even if at inferior quality. Encouraging faculty to cooperate to provide a complete set of courses in a category might follow.[27] After that, allowing students to select from an à la carte menu of courses to complete a degree would be a simple step. If this were accompanied by a joint venture with a degree-granting institution that legitimized the product, entry would be complete.

The advantage of this publisher model would be all the benefits of a distance learning degree plus potentially very low cost. The pricing decision for a course would benchmark off the cost of a book ($60 or $70—a figure close to the per *class* tuition cost at private universities) because all revenue above that is incremental income for the publisher—and the convenience of distance learning.[28]

Again, those of you who disdain the thought of receiving an education almost exclusively through self-studying a book should reflect on how much different the educational experience is from that of many students in large introductory courses—even at the major universities.

Bank of America (Corporate University)

One measure of private sector interest in continuing education is that there are over 1,600 corporate universities in the U.S. today, up from 400 in 1988 (Meister, 1998), serving a total corporate training market of $60 billion and educating 54.5 million students per year. While some universities—like McDonald's U., General Electric's Crotonville, and Motorola, who provides courses for 100,000 employees each year at 100 sites—are well known, others are not so well publicized. This does not reduce their ubiquity. It is estimated that one-third of corporate universities are in companies that employ fewer than 5,000 people, demonstrating that the phenomenon is not confined to large companies. What is perhaps most frightening for traditional universities about their corporate counterparts is that many are intending to sell their services on the open market, with the goal of being 100 percent self-funding. Indeed, 40 percent of Motorola's education budget was already funded by customers and suppliers in 1996 (Meister, 1998).

Corporate universities already play a major role in postsecondary education today, dominating the provision of specific skills training for their own employees. In many ways this is like an old-fashioned apprenticeship, where an employer provides training that was not included during an employee's formal education but is needed for a particular job. However, the entry strategy described here conceives of a corporate university—Bank of America—opening its enrollment to third parties. (I do not actually know whether Bank of America has a corporate university, although I suspect it does.)

The incentive for Bank of America to open classes to outsiders is to generate revenue for an area of the bank that until now has been an expensive overhead cost. Motorola, for example, has a budget of close to $100 million per year in corporate training. Most corporations are today looking to minimize corporate expenses by outsourcing functions or by challenging in-house units to demonstrate their effectiveness by competing on the open market (Collis and Montgomery, 1997). Corporate universities are unlikely to be immune from this pressure, unless they can convince management that the training they provide is a proprietary source of competitive advantage for the bank. While this might be a feasible argument for some higher level courses, basic courses on topics like computer programming and accounting are unlikely to fall in this category.

Entry for Bank of America into the third party education market would be relatively easy. It already has the courses and materials, many of which have been explicitly designed for self-study[29] and which could lead to a certificate in a particular skill. It has the facilities available—not just the campus of the university itself but also the bank branches, which could potentially be used as classrooms after business hours to offer courses in locations that are convenient both to work and home. It has faculty with real-world credentials available from among its own employees. It has a widely recognized brand name that provides instant credibility, at least within a range of banking skills. And it has the extra appeal of being able to offer jobs to graduates from its courses.

Initially entry would focus on specific skills training—mainly basic banking, accounting, computer, and finance courses—but as with the other potential entrants discussed above, a path to sequentially upgrade the product offering is readily apparent. Additional courses in leadership and more general business issues, like marketing, could be offered. Accreditation could be offered by a consortium of banks that recognize one another's courses and might be extended to a range of corporations who collectively legitimize their programs as being equivalent to an MBA. Indeed, firms in the automobile industry in the Detroit area are collaborating to select a set of courses, provided by a variety of universities and other institutions, which they will all recognize.

Regardless of whether corporate universities do end up offering an MBA (which some, such as Arthur D. Little, already do), they threaten to take away from universities some very profitable executive education programs. These might seem to be a small part of university revenue, but I suspect their contribution would be sorely missed.

Other Entrants

Other specialist private sector entrants might include Disney in continuing education. Disney could easily capture part of the alumni market by offering expensive but very upmarket experiential courses, such as woodworking, rock climbing, and photography, at vacation destinations. But Disney could also, over time, migrate from distance learning at the primary and secondary education level, which it entered via educational toys and games, television, and Internet programming, to distance learning for higher education.

Other possible entrants in noneducational parts of the value chain can also contribute to the "deconstruction" of universities. Included here would be professional sports teams launching their own farm teams instead of allowing college teams to make the profit from training; Microsoft acquiring copyrights and making them available on-line to replace the physical library; and Marriott outsourcing the hotel and restaurant functions of the university. Private sector companies increasing their share of research funding would also fall in this category.

Implications

Even if you disagree with the individual strategies I have outlined above, the combination should present a compelling threat.

In fact, I intentionally chose the strategies to paint a picture of the breadth of the threat to universities. Harvard and a small group of elite institutions capture the high end and give instant credibility to new entrants by making their courses available for use; the Open University and other convenience or distance learning entrants capture mature students; Harcourt General and other on-line publishers pick off the low end of the market reselling courses developed by faculty for their own institutions; and Bank of America and the corporate universities take executive education and specific skills training. When the list is extended from these specific names to all the companies of each generic type, the result is the disappearance of huge chunks of the traditionally captive market for universities.

With only a slight exaggeration, it might be possible to assert that the only parts of the traditional educational programs of the university—apart from doctoral training of the next generation of faculty and other advanced degrees—that would be untouched by private sector competition would be the market for residential eighteen-year-olds. This might currently seem a large part of the whole market. After all, a huge share—perhaps up to 75 percent of current income—comes from these students. But how big will that market be when students can choose among a full range of alternatives covering a spectrum of prices? And how high will tuition have to be when all the university's fixed costs have to be covered by the smaller student body?

Indeed, such an education may become a luxury good for the richest class of society, in much the way that the grand European tour functioned at the end of the last century—a dispensable but nevertheless enjoyable diversion; or it may become a rubber stamp, as undergraduate education has become at top-tier universities in Japan.

Strategies for Universities

How can and should universities respond to the threat of private sector intervention? In Collis (1999) I made a number of suggestions to reduce costs and to deal with the deteriorating "six forces" of industry structure. I believe these suggestions are still relevant.

Mitigating rivalry among existing institutions can be achieved by seeking antitrust exemption for a range of practices, from prohibiting merit scholarships to setting tuition rates and faculty salaries. Horizontal differentiation among universities will also help achieve this goal by establishing unique specializations for each institution. If this were accompanied by alliances among universities so that a group collaborated to provide complete coverage, but each alone specialized in a limited set of courses, efficiencies could be gained and competition reduced.

Supplier power can be reduced by ensuring that universities retain the copyright for course materials as well as inventions.[30] Faculty expense can also be controlled by shifting to a compensation scheme that pays separately for teaching and research. Those who do little research would see teaching loads rise under this scenario (or else be replaced by part-timers who only get paid for their teaching), while researchers, particularly those in the social sciences, might have to accept lower salaries because their activities generate no income.

Buyer power can be reduced by universities specializing in particular disciplines because horizontal differentiation reduces student choice within each field, particularly when combined with aggressive marketing of a university's strength in particular areas. Buyer power can also be reduced by pricing a lifetime's education at a low annual rate rather than charging a huge amount for four years.

The viability of substitutes to a university education, such as high school or other nondegree diplomas, can be undermined by public relations campaigns that attack their credibility and by working with industry associations, professional services groups, and employers to maintain the undergraduate degree as the required qualification for employment or further training. More generally, the value of the traditional liberal arts residential undergraduate degree should be reinforced by explaining that it does not so much teach a particular body of knowledge as it educates students how to learn for the rest of their lives. This can be defended more easily if teaching is done through a tutorial system that is hard to replicate on the Web, rather than in huge classes supported by teaching assistants.

Finally, if the intent is to deter entry, strategies such as preventing the accreditation of new institutions and using the ownership of course material copyrights to prevent their widespread dissemination or prohibiting their use at nonuniversity establishments would be appropriate.

However, the biggest change in the past year is the increasing likelihood of effective private sector entry. If that is indeed inevitable, the operative motto becomes "If you can't beat them join them," and the strategic imperative becomes to quickly enter alliances or joint ventures with credible new entrants.

Alliances become an important part of the strategy because success in many of the new businesses requires a set of skills and resources that one institution or company alone is unlikely to possess. While universities have the reputation, faculty, and pedagogical experience, it is more likely that private sector entrants will have the technological know-how, a culture of innovation and experimentation, experience in different channels of distribution, as well as the dollars necessary to invest in somewhat risky enterprises. Separately the two may struggle; together they may well succeed. Alliances also have the benefit of reducing competition. Instead of two players trying to build a strong position in the new market, the joint venture alone is competing for share.

As mentioned above, many of the new entrants, such as the Open University, UNEXT, and several of the distance learning companies, particularly in the business school arena, have made alliances part of their strategy. For them the alliance speeds up the entry process and co-opts a potential opponent. For the university, the alliance provides a cheap way to benefit from the opportunity, as well as a method of ensuring that important business decisions are not held hostage to the vagaries of faculty oversight or votes. The mutual benefit of cooperation in new ventures appears to be so compelling that we can only anticipate their increasing usage.

The need for universities to enter alliances also highlights a second strategic necessity that I believe has become even more important than last year: speed. Once all the good alliance partners have been taken, there are no dance partners left for the wallflowers. More generally, the nature of many of the new markets, particularly those that rely on the Internet, is such that early movers are at a big advantage. As Walter Bauer of the Rand Institute wrote, "For E-learning, as for other sectors of e-commerce, the Internet rewards those who enter early, adapt rapidly, and are ready to seize opportunities as they arise" (Baer, 1999).

As you know, despite their glittering valuations, very nearly all the popular Internet companies, like Amazon.com and E*Trade, lose large sums of money each year as they spend cash in a desperate attempt to accumulate customers faster than competitors.[31] The belief is that only one player will win in each Internet market—the way that Microsoft and AOL have become industry standards—because of the customer loyalty that can be built and the scale economies that can be exploited on-line. While it is not obvious that higher education would ever degenerate into a monopoly, the value of brand name—and the huge fixed cost, low variable cost nature of the new business—suggests that early movers will have sustainable advantages. Conversely, the downward spiral that a late mover can get locked into suggests the penalty for complacency is high.

This implies that universities should attach a great urgency to debates about their future. Rather than sitting back and observing how the market develops, university presidents and administrators should be proactively determining the future of their institutions. Otherwise they will be condemned to be the bystanders that get swept away in the tides of change. And much more than in Collis (1999), I believe those futures must involve an early commitment to enter many of the new market opportunities that are today opening the floodgates of private sector attention and capital. The biggest sin that universities can commit today is of omission not of commission.

Endnotes

1. The chief strategic officer of Sun is keen to publicize the fact that the Internet cuts the variable cost of class time from $300 to $0.03 per hour.
2. One indicator of a potentially disruptive technology is that it initially enters at the low end of a market. Most firms will happily embrace high-end technologies that oversatisfy customer needs and offer high margins. Few embrace seemingly inferior technologies that offer low margins and cannibalize sales of existing profitable products.

3. Currently only one thousand distance-learning degree and certificate courses are listed in *Virtual College: Distance Learning Programs* (Peterson, 1996).

4. Of many current publications on "deconstruction" by BCG, some of the more basic statements are Evans and Wurster (1997, 2000). The success of the notion is exemplified by the annual meeting of the Strategic Management Society, whose theme for 2000 is "Winning Strategies in a Deconstructing World."

5. This raises the ultimate question. If I can get a Harvard education by taking exactly the same courses as if I were attending the university, why go to Harvard? Clearly the argument made about the quality of the peer group would still matter, but how difficult will it be for Internet chat rooms to recreate dorm room conversations? What exactly is intangible about the education that residential students receive? How difficult is it to replicate that educational experience outside the traditional university?

6. It is estimated that one million students will take courses via computer this year (International Data Corporation reported in *Boston Globe*, August 29, 1999, page A22).

7. In 1996 the number was 41 percent; in 1966 it was 15 percent according to the U.S. Census Bureau.

8. College graduates now earn 111 percent more than high school graduates, up from 50 percent in 1980 (Moe, Bailey, and Lau, 1999).

9. According to the U.S. Department of Education, of all undergraduate students in 1995–96, only 13 percent lived on campus and 45 percent were full time, while 36 percent were working full time and 25 percent had children of their own.

10. While 25 percent of individuals considering adult education said distance was a deterrent, 40 percent blamed the time of day courses were offered as a barrier (Moe, Bailey, and Lau, 1999).

11. As I noted in Collis (1999), the increase in leisure time and the length of active retirement also increase demand for a slightly different sort of adult education.

12. By no means have all changes passed by the teaching hospitals. In Boston the two largest Harvard teaching hospitals, Massachusetts General and Brigham and Women's, merged in 1993.

13. Harvard Business School makes tens of millions of dollars "profit" a year from its executive education programs.

14. The following is the argument developed by Frank and Cook (1996).

15. Those of you who doubt this argument should be aware that the primary reason students choose to attend the Harvard Business School is not the educational program (since most students rank learning low on their list of reasons) but the peer network they believe they will build during their two years on campus.

16. The visibility and importance attached to *U.S. News & World Report* rankings exemplifies this dynamic. Schools whose ranking moves up in a particular issue usually experience a substantial increase in applications the following year.

17. Three students from fifty states for four years at $30,000 per year.

18. Note that this might also lead to the deconstruction of universities as they specialize in some areas but reduce or even close down other departments.

19. During the 1960s, for example, the Harvard Business School established or mentored the creation of business schools in Iran, Switzerland, Nicaragua, Costa Rica, and Spain.

20. For a short executive program, which at the Harvard Business School might cost $7,000, the business class flight and hotel accommodation from overseas could easily cost the same again. Providing the course in a company's own location would effectively halve the total

cost of the course. Or, as the CEO of Lotus puts it, "of the $62 billion spent last year on training workers, sixty percent is planes, trains and crappy food" (*Boston Globe,* July 30, 1999, page D1).

21. Joint ventures include Harvard with Pensare, Stanford and Penn with Sylvan Caliber Learning, and Columbia with UNEXT.

22. Calculated as a $60,000 annual salary to pay for four thirty-hour courses each year.

23. One result of this competition will be to pressure all universities to eliminate the research subsidy by more clearly defining a separation between compensation for teaching and research. This can be interpreted as the "deconstruction" of these two activities of the university.

24. One drawback is that all Open University courses were developed for and by the English. Course development customized for the U.S. market is not immediately on the entry strategy agenda.

25. Two examples from the recent Academy of Management meeting include offers from StudyNet to convert original material *even that which is not in digital form* (their italics) for free and from ProQuest to search for articles to accompany a course as well as arrange copyright clearance for those articles.

26. Publishers are already indirect competitors since their provision of ready-made courses substantially reduces the initial investment cost entrants must make in course development.

27. Faculty at a North Carolina nursing school have put together as a private venture a set of materials they have developed at the school that will lead to an accredited associate degree in nursing.

28. In fact, Harcourt intends to charge about the same as a state college, $1,200 per course (Hechinger, 1999).

29. PriceWaterhouseCoopers, for example, has large parts of its basic training for accountants on disk.

30. At what point research, in the sense of personal intellectual development, should become the university's property will ultimately become an issue. If a history professor earns a salary that is more than just compensation for teaching, why should that individual receive the income from the best-selling book she wrote on the French Revolution? At management consulting firms today, for example, individuals who write books based on research performed while at the firm have to give a substantial share of royalties to the firm.

31. Amazon.com is currently losing about $250 million per year. In spite of this, its stock market value is close to $20 billion, and *an announcement* that it was entering the toy business caused its value to appreciate $1.8 billion—close to the total market value of Toys R Us.

References

Baer, W. S. "E-Learning: A Catalyst for Competition in Higher Education." *iMP: Information Impacts Magazine,* June 1999.

Callahan, T. "Go to School." *Parade,* August 1, 1999, p. 4.

Christensen, C. *The Innovator's Dilemma.* Boston: Harvard Business School Press, 1998.

Collis, D. and Montgomery, C. *Corporate Strategy.* Homewood, Ill.: Irwin McGraw, 1997. (See particularly Chapter Six.)

Collis, D. J. "When Industries Change: Scenarios for Higher Education." In J. W. Meyerson and M. Devlin (eds.), *Forum Futures, 1999: Forum Strategy Series, Volume 2*. New Haven, Conn.: Forum for the Future of Higher Education, 1999.

Evans, P. and Wurster, T. *Blown to Bits*. Boston: Harvard Business School Press, 2000.

Evans, P. and Wurster, T. "Strategy and the New Economics of Information." *Harvard Business Review*, 1997 (September/October).

Frank, R. and Cook, P. *The Winner-Take-All Society*. New York: Penguin, 1996.

Hechinger, J. "Textbook Publisher Lays Plan for an Internet University." *Wall Street Journal*, April 11, 1999, p. 1.

Meister, J. *Corporate Universities: Lessons in Building a World-Class Workforce*. New York: McGraw-Hill, 1998.

Moe, M., Bailey K., and Lau, R. *The Book of Knowledge*. New York: Merrill Lynch, 1999.

Peterson Publishing Company, *Virtual College: Distance Learning Programs*. Lawrenceville, N.J.: Peterson Publishing, 1996.

Stone, A., "Business and Education: Learning to Work Together. " *Business Week On-line Briefing*, July 22, 1999.

CHAPTER SEVEN

STRATEGIC AND FINANCIAL PLANNING FOR INFORMATION TECHNOLOGY IN HIGHER EDUCATION

Michael A. McRobbie, Judith G. Palmer

McRobbie and Palmer recognize the potential of technology to bring about major innovations in the entire teaching and learning process. They describe Indiana University's strategic plan for information technology, a comprehensive, university-wide effort that outlines the use of IT in research and academic computing, telecommunications, and administrative support, as well as in teaching and learning. The IT plan is accompanied by a detailed financial plan to help Indiana University meet the enormous fiscal challenges of an enhanced technological environment.

Information technology is fundamental to the teaching, learning, and research missions of modern universities. It is transforming the way universities do business; it is fueling major changes in research, creative activity, and scholarly communication; and it offers the potential for major innovation in the entire teaching and learning process. Information technology has become an essential tool for faculty, students, and staff who use it to organize their ideas, seek information, and communicate with one another and with the world.

"Architecture for the 21st Century: An Information Technology Strategic Plan for Indiana University," published in 1998, outlines in detail Indiana University's strategy for information technology. That strategy for information

Note: We would like to thank Gerry Bernbom and Laurie Antolovic of the Office of the Vice President for Information Technology and Chief Information Officer and Stephen L. Keucher and Arthur J. Lindeman of the Office of the Vice President and Chief Financial Officer, all at Indiana University, for their valuable contributions to this paper.

technology must fit into the institution's broader strategic plan. Indiana University (IU) operates under a university-wide plan, The Strategic Directions Charter, comprising thirty major recommendations that address three broad themes:

- Establishing communities of learning
- Implementing methods of accountability and best practices
- Meeting the responsibilities of excellence

Established in 1994 under the leadership of IU President Myles Brand, this initiative has resulted in $25 million allocated as seed funds for projects addressing the priorities outlined in the Charter.

In his 1997 State of the University address, President Brand set a challenge for Indiana University "to take the next step in institutional academic excellence and move into the very top tier of the nation's public universities." IU's strategy for information technology is a direct response to this challenge, to rise to a position of absolute leadership among public universities in the creative use and application of information technology (IT). The creation of new knowledge and the sharing of information are defining features of a modern university; thus the goal of excellence in the use of IT is an essential ingredient in achieving academic excellence for the institution as a whole.

Information Technology at Indiana University

Institutional leadership for information technology at Indiana University is the responsibility of the Office of the Vice President for Information Technology. The portfolio of this office includes University Information Technology Services (UITS) on the Bloomington and Indianapolis campuses, as well as the chief information officers positions on IU's five smaller campuses.

University Information Technology Services, with offices on the Bloomington and Indianapolis campuses, is responsible for the development of a modern information technology environment throughout the university in support of IU's vision for excellence in research, teaching, outreach, and lifelong learning. UITS comprises some 500 highly trained professionals with expertise that spans the field of information technology, plus 500 additional part-time employees. Many of the staff are nationally and internationally known for their accomplishments.

Central information technology services are supported with an annual budget of approximately $70 million. These funds come from four chief sources: central university funds, the Bloomington campus, the Indianapolis campus, and the regional campuses. Above these base funds, there is in the current biennium direct state funding to IU of approximately $21 million per year designated for IT, with the intent on the part of the state to continue direct funding. There is also $7 million in state funding dedicated to high-speed networking. Additionally, IU currently has external or grant funding for information technology in excess of $40 million.

Information technology is central to a number of academic endeavors at IU: computer science, information science, engineering and technology; the physical, biological, and social sciences; medicine and the health sciences; and the arts and humanities. In the past year IU launched its first new academic school in over twenty-five years, the School of Informatics, and began enrolling students in its program in new media. Research at IU is conducted in artificial intelligence, cognitive science, robotics, high performance computing, logic and programming languages, and a number of fields that are influenced and enabled through information technology.

In 1999, IU received a gift of $30 million from the Lilly Endowment to establish the Indiana Pervasive Computing Research (IPCRES) initiative, a major research and development effort focused on some of the fundamental technologies that will drive the twenty-first century information economy. This is the largest gift ever received by Indiana University.

The IPCRES initiative builds on IU's accomplishments in information technology in order to advance a program of basic research in software technologies and advanced telecommunications that will underlie pervasive computing. The overall strategy of IPCRES will be to significantly expand IT research in Indiana, specifically in pervasive computing, and leverage this research to expand the information economy in Indiana. Both activities—basic research and support for economic development—are fundamental to the mission of a public research university.

Key to this initiative will be establishment of six world-class research laboratories in areas fundamental to building the pervasive computing environment of the future. These IPCRES laboratories will be headed by researchers of the highest international standing, distinguished scientists recognized as leaders in their respective fields, who will attract highly talented young faculty and graduate students to join them.

As part of its overall strategy, IPCRES will leverage this research effort to expand the information economy in Indiana. Establishment of an economic development office will be central to these efforts. The goal of this office is to build on the technology developments and scientific discoveries of the IPCRES laboratories to create new businesses, to infuse new technologies into existing businesses, and to attract new companies to Indiana. It will also build on IU's involvement in national and international developments in advanced telecommunications and software technologies that will underpin pervasive computing. IU is home to a number of world-class research programs in these areas, is centrally involved in Internet2 and a number of major international research networks, and has strong relationships with leading IT companies such as IBM, Microsoft, and Cisco.

IU's investments in information technology recognize and build on the strengths of IU as a multicampus institution with a formidable reputation in the arts, humanities, social sciences, basic sciences, and health sciences, and with an increasing emphasis on technology and applied science.

The Information Technology Strategic Plan

Indiana University's Information Technology Strategic Plan is the most comprehensive and far-reaching plan ever prepared for the development of information technology at IU. The plan is university-wide in scope, covering a period of six years, from 1998 to 2004.

The strategic plan outlines the use of IT in research and academic computing, teaching and learning, telecommunications, and administrative support. It recognizes the transformational power of IT in higher education and the pace of technological change, which call for flexibility and experimentation in every phase of IT planning and implementation.

The plan was developed through a five-month period of intensive effort, from January to May 1998, through the dedicated work of the University Information Technology Committee and four advisory task forces. Broad input was received from faculty, staff, and students across all IU campuses, including the campus IT councils at Bloomington and Indianapolis and the campus computing center directors.

Two major themes are woven throughout the ten major recommendations of the plan. The first is access. The plan should lead to improved access to information, computation, and communication for students, faculty, and staff. The second is life-cycle funding. The plan should put in place a reliable mechanism to sustain innovation through ongoing replacement and upgrading of information technology. The primacy of these themes is reflected in the strategic plan's recommendations.

IT Strategic Plan Recommendations

1. Build a solid foundation of IT infrastructure and assure that sound fiscal planning permits maintenance of this infrastructure at state-of-the-art levels. A standard amount per year must be budgeted to support life-cycle replacement

of equipment and to assure appropriate levels of technical support for faculty, students, and staff.

2. Students, faculty, and staff should be provided with reliable access to computing and network services, on and off the campuses. The electronic borders between home, community, workplace, and campus should become invisible, at little or no additional cost over current telephone technology.

3. Incentives and support should be offered so that faculty and staff are encouraged in the creative use and application of information technology for teaching, research, and service. Tenure and promotion guidelines, merit reviews, fellowships, and grants all present means for helping faculty and staff move along the IT learning curve.

4. The university should assume a position of worldwide leadership in the use of IT to facilitate and enhance teaching and learning. There are numerous ways in which IT can enhance teaching and learning, particularly by increasing access to resources and increasing the quality of instructional methods.

5. To support research, the university should provide broad backing for basic collaboration technologies and begin implementing more advanced technologies. Advanced data storage and high-performance computing services, for example, are crucial to the ongoing support of university research.

6. Institutional information systems should be prioritized, so that they work together in a seamless manner and accommodate an ever-increasing number of users. Common interfaces and a common information delivery environment must be implemented to facilitate the integrated use of data.

7. Plans for a converged telecommunications infrastructure must be accelerated. The convergence of voice, video, and data technologies promise great savings and important new services if harnessed in a timely and effective manner.

8. The university must provide IT tools, infrastructure, and support services to students so that they may effectively engage in learning and research. This includes technology support centers and a seamless computing environment that crosses the borders between campus, home, and residence halls.

9. The digital library program should be expanded and a digital library infrastructure should be developed to support research, teaching, and learning. IT has transformed the availability of resources; state-of-the-art libraries and professional librarians will be invaluable in helping the university community manage and mine the unprecedented amounts of digital information accessible today.

10. Policies and procedures must be developed to protect the security of IT resources and data, safeguard personal privacy, and ensure that intellectual

property rights are respected. At the same time, traditional values associated with academic freedom, including access to information and freedom of discourse, must be preserved and promoted.

Implementing the IT Strategic Plan

Each of the ten major recommendations in the Indiana University IT Strategic Plan, states an overarching goal and vision, accompanied by a number of specific actions intended to achieve that vision. Exhibit 7.1 expands on recommendation 4 related to teaching and learning, by listing several examples of supporting actions.

The IT Strategic Plan was presented to the university president and board of trustees in June 1998. There followed then a period of far-reaching consultation within the university. During the fall semester of 1998, more than fifty briefings on the plan were held for faculty councils, advisory committees, campus chancellors and their senior staffs, student organizations, and others. Input and comment were requested and advice as to priorities was particularly sought. The results of these briefings were overwhelmingly positive, and the recommendations and priorities of the IT Strategic Plan received the strongest possible endorsement from the IU community.

Also during the fall semester, senior staff in the Office of the Vice President for Information Technology developed a preliminary estimate of the budget required for full implementation of the IT Strategic Plan. Successive versions of this budget were reviewed by the Office of the Vice President and Chief Financial Officer who initiated the process of securing state funding for this undertaking. This budget estimated the cost of each individual action in the plan, identified onetime and ongoing expenses, determined how the expenditure of funds would be allocated among the campuses and across the major organizational divisions of research and academic computing, teaching and learning information technologies, telecommunications, and university information systems. Accompanying the budget was a preliminary implementation plan for each of the ten recommendations and sixty-eight actions in the IT Strategic Plan. This budget and implementation plan was presented to the IU president and board of trustees in December 1998. With their approval, implementation began in earnest in January 1999.

The implementation plan involved the continuation of many ongoing activities, the reshaping or refining of some existing activities and services, and the development of a number of new initiatives and programs. The plan did not presume that all funding needed for implementation would come from the central

EXHIBIT 7.1.   IT STRATEGIC PLANNING AND TEACHING AND LEARNING INFORMATION TECHNOLOGY

RECOMMENDATION: It is a goal of the IT Strategic Plan that Indiana University should assume a position of worldwide leadership in the use of information technology to facilitate and enhance teaching and learning. Information technology will facilitate and enhance teaching and learning by

- Improving access to the teaching resources of Indiana University
- Eliminating or reducing constraints due to time, place, method of instruction, or format of traditional university calendars
- Supporting and promoting the preparation of quality instructional content for use with information technology
- Fostering greater teacher and student interaction and promoting active student engagement
- Supporting more varieties of instructional formats
- Increasing access to information resources through the library and World Wide Web
- Providing "help desk" services to support asynchronous learning
- Creating a seamless environment for the development of a genuine distributed learning community for both students and faculty

Some specific actions to support this recommendation include the following:

- The Teaching and Learning Technology Lab and the Center for Teaching and Learning should be expanded, and new services developed where needed, to offer standard-level teaching support services for all faculty at Bloomington, Indianapolis, and the regional campuses.
- To support course tools development and initiatives in distributed education, UITS (through its Advanced Information Technology Laboratory) should evaluate Web-based and other network-based learning environments and offer faculty a comprehensive set of options to easily create, edit, revise, and maintain on-line course material.
- The university should offer, on a selective basis, intensive help in developing instructional material for delivery to IU students, for eventual offering as a marketable IU product, or both.
- The university should provide overall guidelines and direct support to help facilitate relationships with publishers for the commercial development and marketing of technology-based instructional materials.
- UITS should evaluate the opportunities to partner with faculty in the sciences to experiment with simulation-based laboratory courses and should be alert to other possible partnerships for the enhancement of instruction through simulation and visualization.

(continued)

EXHIBIT 7.1.   IT STRATEGIC PLANNING AND TEACHING AND LEARNING INFORMATION TECHNOLOGY *(continued)*

- To support existing and emerging faculty initiatives in basic skills education, the university should explore the use of IT to aid in the teaching of these basic skills.
- UITS, with the new associate vice president for distributed education, should help coordinate initiatives in distributed education, by helping departments and schools implement new programs, without duplicating existing services. UITS should continue to assist programs of distributed education, helping to identify supported and supportable technologies that can satisfy their complex requirements.
- UITS should ensure an available and reliable infrastructure of networks, servers, storage, and applications for the support of on-line courses and other new learning experiences.
- UITS should initiate changes to university information systems that improve the quality of instruction, service to students, or manageability of the distributed education program itself.

Implementation plans were developed for each individual action item above and for all sixty-eight actions recommended in the IT Plan.

Source: "Architecture for the 21st Century: An Information Technology Strategic Plan for Indiana University," available at http://www.indiana.edu/~ovpit/strategic/. For a recent progress report on accomplishments toward these and other actions in the IT Plan, see "UITS Accomplishments Report," 1999–2000, http://www.indiana.edu/~uits/cpo/accomplish/.

IT organization or from any single source. Each action and recommendation in the IT Strategic Plan was evaluated to determine

Which had resources already committed to their accomplishment

Which offered partnership opportunities to pool central resources with campus or departmental resources

Which required new allocation or reallocation of resources, either centrally or across the campuses, schools and departments.

It was clear from this analysis that new funds, reallocation of existing funds, and continued investments in current initiatives would all be necessary.

The implementation plan developed by the Office of the Vice President for Information Technology proposed a number of strategies for allocating funds:

Central base funding of central services

Using central funds to match campus or departmental funds for distributed services

Onetime seed funding for the start-up of new services

Temporary "bridge" funding to allow for the transition to local base funding

In addition, some IT services may be funded through user fees or through direct funding at the individual campus level.

This implementation plan formed the basis for detailed logistical planning within the IT organization and across the schools and campuses, and for detailed financial planning with the Office of the Vice President and Chief Financial Officer and with the various campus financial officers.

Financial Planning Challenges

Planning for information technology presents universities and colleges with enormous financial challenges. Nearly every institutional program and office, both academic and administrative, has the potential to be affected by information technology. The rapidly changing pace of technological development intensifies the breadth of this impact. Without careful planning, an institution can quickly exceed its capacity to support the financial demands of this enhanced technological environment. Any IT strategic plan should be accompanied by sound fiscal analysis of the estimated expenditure requirements, time horizons for implementation, activity and funding priorities, and alternative resource support possibilities.

A sound financial plan will allow the institution to see that its IT goals are achievable, moving the discourse from a perception of dreams to the reality of achievements. A thoughtful and clearly stated financial plan with achievable goals will increase stakeholder interest and decrease anxieties about inequitable funding distributions and reallocation burdens. It will also assure that the institution recognizes the potential of leveraging new resources.

From a budgetary perspective, a successful IT funding plan will not only incorporate existing resource allocations for technology, but it also will address whether these dollars can be better leveraged by more centralized decision making about expenditures. An IT funding plan should also identify institutional reallocations that can result from improved utilization of technology, which will be most effective when combined with reengineering opportunities formulated to enhance performance and efficiencies. One of the important aspects of the institutional IT plan is the information systems (IS) component. The IS plan, with the full support of the IT infrastructure investments, provides the institution with the capability of reengineering its business activities. The technologies and institutional policies that contribute most are collaborative in nature: e-mail, transaction processing portals, electronic documents, information databases, and the World Wide Web.

An example of how an institution can leverage a technology investment to achieve real workforce and process reengineering may be helpful to underscore the point. When Indiana University implemented its new financial information system in July 1994, the Financial Management Services Office undertook a significant reengineering effort designed to upgrade the skills of its workforce, while at the same time changing its actual activities from transaction processing functions to compliance monitoring and analysis. These changes required the staff to be more highly trained but smaller than the previous staff, which had performed a number of data input functions. Skill enhancement and administrative performance improvements were felt throughout the institution.

Simply improving the technology, however, was not sufficient in itself to fully justify the investment; it was also necessary to ensure that work patterns and skill sets were changed to reflect the enhanced processing and information system. The richness of the information environment and the timeliness of the data available served to upgrade overall institutional management. Finally, it was important to ensure customer satisfaction.

Involvement with several other administrative operations from across the university was crucial during the transition. To assist university deans and administrative directors in improving their financial and operational performance, the output quality of the unit was reviewed and assessed, along with a cost analysis and overall financial evaluation. Once this step in the process is completed, there is a much higher likelihood that the visioning and planning processes can lead to meaningful policy changes and cost revisions. At Indiana University, we call this process the "Economic Model," but it has its roots in activity-based costing principles. By examining our changing economic environment and exploring new frameworks for decision making, we have been successful in using our new IT tools in helping schools and campuses adapt to changing expectations. We have been careful to include those responsible for internal and external auditing—auditors were fully integrated into the team to ensure that appropriate control and separation of duties standards were maintained in the new system as well as in the new workforce arrangements.

The tendency for technological changes to be viewed as simply new applications or additions to existing operations must be recognized and countered. The tendency often becomes evident when the cost of operations after the implementation of a new system is estimated. When a unit's financial analysis projects significant increases in staffing requirements as a result of new technologies, it may be a signal that the unit is not taking full advantage of the technology to change the way that work is managed.

It is important to be realistic in the cost saving expectations associated with a new information technology investment. At least two benchmarks can be used to measure results. The first is to quantify any actual reductions in costs for a specific process or function. Most likely this will be measured in terms of the number of people involved in accomplishing a certain task, although there may be areas where an actual process or portion thereof may be eliminated completely. Second, the use of technology often will accomplish the same objective with less human capital investment. Many good examples of the latter can be cited in the development of e-commerce or e-business opportunities. In these instances, savings accrue from technological investments even though the activity levels associated with the function may not expand.

This review process also allows the university to measure potential financial benefits accruing from the implementation of new systems and technologies. Focusing for a moment on the information systems side of IT—though the techniques apply equally well to some academic processes—we have discovered that activity-based costing techniques often reveal hidden expenses associated with administrative procedures, thus providing management with a better understanding of the true costs associated with a specific activity. This is a logical first step in determining the current actual cost, so that an accurate measurement of cost savings from new technology systems can be calculated. Of course, it is difficult to track and measure productivity gains. As is the case with most universities, Indiana University struggles with how to measure performance and compare its operations with those of similar institutions. We continue to work toward defining credible productivity metrics so that the university can properly evaluate its investments and performance.

The benefits of IT and other reengineering investments take a long time, perhaps a year or more, to manifest themselves. Further, some investments in information technology may result in short-term cost increases resulting from a number of factors, including the expense of developmental efforts. However, it is important to monitor and manage these effectively so that the long-term results are beneficial to the overall financial condition of the institution. Rather than assuming that technology will result in decreased base costs for all activities, the IT plan should focus on the ability of technology to restrain future long-term costs of the institutions. Although we have just begun, the information technology investments have already enabled Indiana University to improve the integration of decentralized operations and minimize the effects of organizational fragmentation.

New technology can help to control costs in growth areas. For example, the successful implementation of the university's new financial information system enabled the office performing post–award contract and grant compliance to reduce its staff by nearly 18 percent during a time when grant and contract activity increased more than 38 percent. Effective use of technology, process reengineering, and professional staff development resulted in a significant increase in overall productivity in this area.

In all likelihood a broad based information technology plan will require additional support in the form of onetime initial outlays, as well as ongoing base cost increases. It is important to distinguish between these two expenses; only then will an institution be able to design a strategy that most appropriately meets its needs and seek additional support for technology investments. For public institutions additional support may require working with appropriate governmental agencies to secure additional public support. For both public and independent institutions, other possible funding initiatives might include increasing efforts to secure endowments, gifts, and grants; consideration of increases in student fees; and enhancing partnership activities with corporations and other institutions and agencies.

It is imperative for institutions to begin to think differently about their finance and budget planning with respect to information technology. For example, in order to assure life-cycle funding, the barriers of existing financial structures must be significantly altered to guarantee that necessary funding will be available. It is likely that some new procedures will need to be developed to facilitate internal matching opportunities between existing unit budgets. Certainly it is expected that overall investments in technology will increase significantly and, in most institutions, it is expected that technology expenditures will grow more rapidly than overall budgets generally. Figure 7.1 graphically displays this phenomenon for Indiana University's general fund operating budget.

FIGURE 7.1.   INDIANA UNIVERSITY INVESTMENTS IN TECHNOLOGY: COMPARISON OF CHANGES IN TECHNOLOGY EXPENDITURES AND OPERATING BUDGET

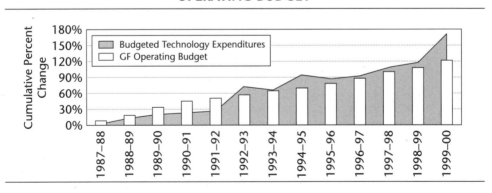

Moreover, institutions need to develop budget and expenditure tracking systems to assist decision makers in determining how an institution is expending its technology investment and where such expenditures are occurring. Figure 7.2 is a snapshot of Indiana University's current investments in technology. With the increasing pressure on hiring and retaining staff skilled in the technological fields, it can be assumed that a larger share of the budget will soon be devoted to human resource needs.

The human resource shortage in IT presents a challenge that threatens the most thorough planning. Higher salaries, greater incentives, and bonus structures are needed to attract and retain high quality IT staff; such incentives may be necessary even though they are outside broader institutional compensation plans. One element of a plan for human resources is to grow and retain IT talent internally, but even then retention of these staff will remain problematic.

Finally, even though institutions will make every effort to accommodate the needs of technology within normal budgeting and financing strategies, it is reasonable to assume that many institutions will have to seek outside longer term financing opportunities, particularly as needs for significant up-front investments in systems are required. Traditional capital financing markets do not lend themselves to short- and medium-term financing for most institutions. The effective asset life for many technological investments falls far short of the traditional asset life definition. As evidence of the complexity of categorizing technological investments, it is increasingly difficult to assign these investments to the standard operating and capital classifications. It may be necessary for higher education

FIGURE 7.2.   INDIANA UNIVERSITY INVESTMENTS IN TECHNOLOGY: ALLOCATIONS FY 2000

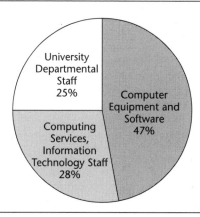

institutions and capital financing organizations to come together to consider possible strategies that would allow for the amortization of these costs. Just as institutions are being asked to think differently about the way they perform their work, we may need to ask the greater financial community to consider new strategies with regard to financing technological development.

Conclusion

Colleges and universities must recognize the transforming influence of information technology. IT permeates every aspect of the university, from ubiquitous desktop computers, to the intricate web of fiber optic cables that link these computers to the world of digital information, to the wired classrooms, dormitories, and laboratories that have become critical components of the processes of education and research.

To most effectively harness the possibilities IT presents, institutions will best be served by articulating their unique identities and building on their strengths, so that their IT strategic plans align with their institutional visions and missions. Strategic plans should reflect institutional priorities; colleges and universities should thoughtfully consider IT needs in light of their institutional missions and should engage the academic community throughout the planning process. While the strategic paths chosen today will vary across institutions, the choice of these paths will be critical in setting the direction and trajectory for technological change in the decades to come.

Resources

"Architecture for the 21st Century: An Information Technology Strategic Plan for Indiana University." [http://www.indiana.edu/~ovpit/strategic/], May 1998.

IPCRES: Indiana Pervasive Computing Research Initiative. [http://www.indiana.edu/~ovpit/ipcres/], September 1999.

Office of the Vice President and Chief Financial Officer. [http://www.indiana.edu/~vpcfo/].

Office of the Vice President for Information Technology and Chief Information Officer. [http://www.indiana.edu/~ovpit/].

CHAPTER EIGHT

WHY SOME ENTERPRISE IMPROVEMENT MODELS HAVE MORE LASTING EFFECTS THAN OTHERS

Wendell C. Brase

Brase presents a model for effecting behavioral change leading to improved organizational performance that can be sustained over time. The model is based on empirical research showing that the primary role of effective managers is to foster workplace respect, which enables workplace cooperation, which in turn yields organizational performance. Brase's research indicates that key managerial behaviors—including the ones that seem more like traits than acquired skills—can be codified, measured, and learned.

Many process improvement models are behaviorally naive—heavy on the rhetoric of "teamwork," "empowerment," "new paradigms," and "accountability" but lacking insight into workplace belief systems, values, motivations, and disincentives that underlie the behaviors targeted for change. Some management change programs are precise and detailed about process redesign methods but vague and conceptual about behavioral dynamics. Sometimes they express behavioral expectations through new jargon or preachy admonitions, both readily construed by employees as "you're not doing it right." These actually *thwart* lasting change, although people may wisely adopt the new parlance rather than appear out of step with the change program. Such models are unsophisticated about how to stimulate fundamental, *sustainable* change in the way an enterprise does its business.

Too Many Good Ideas

The decade extending from about 1985 to 1995 saw a plethora of popular management books that advocated a variety of dogmas. Managers were urged to promote teamwork through reward systems and new organization forms, to pay for performance, to train managers and staff in total quality principles, to deploy cross-functional teams to reengineer core business processes, to return to value-based management fundamentals, to adopt the Baldridge criteria, to foster and reward continuous improvement, to implement balanced scorecards, to derive and use customer-driven performance measures, to benchmark these measures, and to employ all these strategies while downsizing, outsourcing, simplifying, and producing just-in-time results. No manager could employ *all* these programs without a large staff and an ample budget. Some management improvement programs that advocated simplification, streamlining, clarity, and accountability became obese, rigid, and even bureaucratic, violating their own precepts. The streamlining agenda needed a dose of its own medicine, although most enterprise improvement programs did not contemplate that improvements might need to be reflected back on the program methodology itself.

Moreover, conscientious managers had little objective information to enable them to choose from an array of rapidly promulgated ideas. Most "new ideas" in management were backed by little verifiable data demonstrating their efficacy. Many ideas were superbly presented not only in print but also by consultants who polished and added pricey legitimacy. Most new methods were promoted without attacking other strategies but with a dogmatism that implied the superiority of new theories over their antecedents and competing models. Anecdotal evidence was used to extol new methods of organizing, managing, and rewarding people, buoyed by rising (warranted) optimism about the productivity and international competitiveness of American industries. However, the individual manager had insufficient evidence about the relative effectiveness of various improvement programs to enable an informed decision about where best to invest limited time. Which tools would lead most efficiently and assuredly to improved enterprise performance?

In fact, many of the enterprise improvement programs that surfaced (or *re*surfaced) in the past decade were unvalidated models. They may sound sensible and appear to yield measurable benefits, but there is limited evidence—in terms of systematic cause and effect—to link management actions with desired group behaviors (such as teamwork, collaboration, and information sharing) or with overall organizational performance.

The Irvine Management Change Model

The University of California, Irvine's "Model for Sustaining Administrative Improvement" (http://www.abs.uci.edu/depts/vcabs/toc.html) was similarly unvalidated. This program—recognized by the National Association of College and University Business Officers (Higher Education Awards Program first prize, 1996), by *USA Today* (1998 Quality Cup Award), and by a 1997 CAUSE (association for managing information resources in higher education) Best Practices Award—produced numerous process improvements and productivity results. However, no statistical evidence demonstrated that the program's normative elements correlated with desired organizational performance or with long-term change in the "administrative culture."

As a program dedicated to sustained, rather than episodic, improvement, UC Irvine's Model for Sustaining Administrative Improvement contained distinct, value-based behavioral components. These elements were considered necessary to change the patterns of a bureaucracy through altering the dynamic of values, expectations, rewards, disincentives, and belief systems that define and perpetuate the administrative culture of an institution.

The Irvine model contains explicit normative elements in three areas:

- *Teamwork principles,* increasingly needed as the organization becomes less hierarchical and more networked, wherein process improvement becomes increasingly cross-functional
- *Simplification goals and principles,* designed to counter the inherent tendencies of a bureaucracy to add systems, program-variants, controls, specialized policies, and layers of complexity
- *Effectiveness principles,* comprising quality criteria expressing accountability and performance values that differ sharply from prior shared beliefs, conventional wisdom, and bureaucratic patterns

These principles are intentionally crafted to alter values and status quo behaviors that have become comfortable. Bureaucracies' internal dynamics create strong drives to preserve or return to status quo conditions in the face of change. These dynamics, rooted in rule-making and enforcement behavior, are typically entrenched because status quo practices embedded in policy allow accountability and responsibility to be comfortably fragmented in ways that are "safe." Such a system is stable and predictable in its behavior, yet is inefficient when conditions shift and unresponsive when change is needed.

Individual, Group, and Supervisor Performance Expectations

The Irvine Model for Sustaining Administrative Improvement expressed norma-tive behaviors for individuals, teams, and supervisors. Teamwork, simplification, and effectiveness principles and values were taught in workshops, incorporated in performance evaluation criteria, expressed in organizational goals, rewarded through incentive compensation, acknowledged through publicity and internal recognition, operationalized through delegated authorities, measured in numer-ous ways, and embodied in guidelines that were posted in the workplace. Systems, policies, and practices that ran counter to the model's normative elements were dismantled or changed.

Since an administrative culture derives, in part, from workplace values, beliefs, expectations, and rewards that are embedded in human resources policies and practices, human resources programs were addressed early, as a foundation element in the model. For example, classification of management positions had rewarded bigger budgets, hierarchical layering, and organizational complexity. Analysis also revealed that some managers were reluctant to pursue downsizing, restructuring, or outsourcing due to classification disincentives or concern about the university's (prior) mediocre track record in reemploying displaced staff. Finally, performance evaluation did not reinforce team behavior, innovation, and process streamlining to the extent needed for consistent support of campus administra-tive improvement goals. Therefore, as foundational elements—due to their precursor role—a reemployment program was instituted to enhance placement opportunities for laid-off staff, a "size-neutral" position classification system was introduced (removing such factors as number of staff, size of budget, and number of reporting levels below a position under consideration), and the performance evaluation form and incentive award program were revised to emphasize process improvement, innovation, and teamwork.

The Irvine Model for Sustaining Administrative Improvement included goals for reduction in the number of administrative systems and system-variants, productivity targets in four service units, goals for benchmarking and importing exemplary practices, and customer-driven performance measures. Implementing the model required process improvement projects throughout the organization. Teamwork was essential, in terms of both team-based problem solving and team behavior in everyday cooperation.

The envisioned organizational effectiveness was rooted in shared values characterized by particular desired patterns:

- No one is rewarded for (intentionally) looking good at the expense of another. Team players are committed to each other's success.

- Teamwork requires willingness on the part of individuals to enter into interdependencies involving risk, which require a foundation of trust. Supervisory practices, rewards, recognitions, and performance measurement systems must not undermine interdependencies or trust between individuals.
- Innovation requires open debate about many "wrong" ideas. Complex process redesign starts with creative chaos and early mistakes in order to avoid *late*-stage errors. Management must make it comfortable to be "wrong" at the beginning of problem solving.
- Teams are empowered to solve problems (rather than merely *advise* a manager's solution).
- Respect for facts, data, and objective analysis fosters teamwork. People are more willing to create interdependencies involving trust and vulnerability when they feel that facts and neutral data are valued.
- A less authoritarian hierarchy reduces the risk-exposure of competent individuals, enabling them to enter into interdependencies because their ideas can be expressed through fewer layers that might involve filtering or inadvertent distortion. Misunderstandings can be corrected more readily in a less hierarchical organization.
- Interpersonal problems are resolved effectively—limiting the degree to which they undermine teamwork by distorting perceptions of others' motives, which tends to occur when stakeholders struggle with change.
- Supervisors and coworkers value innovation, continuous improvement, and a willingness to question and improve on the status quo.

These values and desired dynamics were operationalized into eleven normative workplace patterns that could be stated as simple performance expectations, fostered through training, included (to varying degrees) as performance criteria in evaluation tools and reward systems, and measured through employee surveys:

1. People who seek better methods are respected and rewarded.
2. People experience a climate of mutual respect in the workplace.
3. Groups value member suggestions, including ones that are initially "wrong."
4. Coworkers produce ideas that help solve problems when they surface.
5. Problems with the way the group does its work are faced and addressed.
6. Members can criticize the way the work group functions without penalty.
7. People can discuss problems without fear of looking stupid to coworkers.
8. Interpersonal conflicts are addressed and resolved in the work group.
9. Differences of opinion about how to get the job done are discussed openly.

10. Differences of opinion about how to get the job done are resolved using facts.
11. Everyone shares responsibility for the results of group tasks (not just the supervisor or a few key participants).

Do Management Behaviors Affect Teamwork and Cooperation?

A number of supervisory behaviors and values were articulated in the model because they were expected to reinforce the desired organizational performance, as discussed above. These were expressed as performance expectations and incorporated into performance evaluations, reward criteria, management development workshops, and stated objectives. Although these performance expectations were considered worthwhile on their own merits, it was important to discover whether they reinforce teamwork, problem solving, and organizational effectiveness.

In order to research this question, employees were surveyed across the administrative services organization of the University of California, Irvine. They evaluated their work groups in terms of the patterns, behaviors, and values highlighted above, and evaluated their supervisors in terms of numerous traits and behaviors. This survey has been administered three times over the past three years, with response rates ranging from 51 to 70 percent.

Management Effectiveness Model Analysis of survey responses revealed very strong correlations between many management behaviors and organizational effectiveness, and with desired group patterns of open communications, trust, and collaborative problem solving. Further analysis (with the assistance of the UC Irvine Center for Statistical Consulting) suggested a multistage causal model of the structure shown in Figure 8.1.

The management behaviors that evidenced strength in this model fell into four general categories.

First, supervisors are ethically and emotionally consistent. They

- Model behavior they expect from others
- Communicate honestly with employees
- Keep promises and commitments to employees
- Make important decisions based on the organization's best interests
- Act in ways that build employees' respect
- Base their actions on a consistent set of principles
- Earn employees' trust

Second, supervisors communicate respect for employees. Supervisors

- Communicate clear expectations
- Trust subordinates' judgment
- Take time to listen and understand employee views

FIGURE 8.1.   MANAGEMENT EFFECTIVENESS MODEL

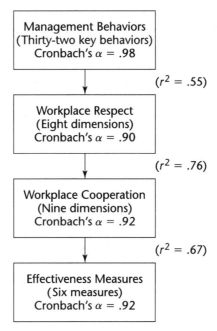

$N \cong 175$ (varies based on questions' response rates)

- Help employees understand "the bigger picture"
- Show respect when communicating
- Care about employees as individuals
- Involve employees in developing objectives, performance measures, and plans
- Do *not* gain advantage by holding back information
- Do *not* make employees feel stupid when they disagree

Third, supervisors accept responsibility and act on it, in that they

- Take steps to improve bad interpersonal relationships
- Accept constructive criticism without becoming defensive
- Reward the best performers
- Make good decisions despite incomplete information
- Admit mistakes and move on
- Separate vital tasks from less important ones
- Do the most important tasks first
- Accept responsibility if things go wrong, rather than blame others

Fourth, supervisors are open-minded and are team players. Supervisors

- Work well with their peers
- Support equal opportunity
- Seek a range of views when solving problems
- Value perspectives from people of diverse backgrounds
- Tend to find win-win solutions
- Encourage employees to surface problems
- Will praise an effort that was promising even if it failed
- Do *not* make some people look good at others' expense

The workplace respect measures included:

- People who seek better ways of doing things are respected and rewarded
- Members can criticize the way the work group functions without penalty
- People can discuss problems without fear of looking stupid to coworkers
- Coworkers experience a climate of mutual respect
- Coworkers recognize and accept each other's strengths and weaknesses
- Coworkers share leadership responsibilities and often hand off leadership roles
- Work groups face and attend to problems with the way work is performed
- Coworkers address and resolve interpersonal conflicts

The workplace cooperation construct comprised:

- Groups value members' suggestions, including ones that are initially "wrong"
- Coworkers produce ideas that help solve problems
- Everyone shares responsibility for team results
- Groups experience *fewer* interpersonal problems when stressed
- Work group members share a common set of work goals
- Work group members share the same standards of effectiveness
- Work group members share values of service, quality, and excellence
- Coworkers share expertise when confronting a new problem
- Work group members are unconcerned about whether tasks are distributed equitably

Finally, effectiveness measures encompassed:

- Work groups tackle problems *before* complaints are received
- Work groups continually improve practices, productivity, and effectiveness
- Work groups are committed to meeting customers' needs

- Work groups rate themselves as efficient and productive
- Work groups rate their quality and productivity "usually very good" or "consistently excellent"
- Work groups report that customers rate their performance "usually very good" or "consistently outstanding."

The Value of Coherence Within Variable Constructs

The constructs of management behaviors, workplace respect, and workplace cooperation variables are tightly clustered, with strong intercorrelations ($\alpha > .90$). This suggests that employees view these variables as part of a coherent experience.

Consistency and coherence are essential attributes of any management change model that aims to change an administrative culture. When people sense even the slightest inconsistency in the new rules of the game, they retreat to the safety of status quo behaviors. Coherence calls for a complete, integrated set of goals, foundations, and tools. Coherence in a management change model means that no essential pieces are missing and that all components of the model—symbols, premises, implicit values, rewards, communications, improvement tools, and protocols—are painstakingly consistent, with no mixed messages. The reliability coefficients that characterize the model's constructs provide evidence of consistency and coherence.

How to Interpret This Model

The management change model diagrammed above is remarkably simple, and its interpretation is therefore straightforward. Although correlation analysis does not enable the assignment of predictive or causal arrows, they are hypothesized as follows: management behaviors provide the *foundation* (or lack thereof) for workplace respect; this cluster of measures is, in turn, the precursor to workplace cooperation, which then leads to effectiveness measures. The primary effect of management behaviors is on workplace respect, which appears to *enable* workplace cooperation, which then yields team-based performance.

The model demonstrates the foundational role of management in enabling teamwork and collaboration, since certain supervisory behaviors are essential to foster workplace respect—the necessary precursor to patterns of workplace cooperation. The model reveals a singular, critical-path linearity; partial correlations of other possible relationships approach zero. Analysis of the "third generation" survey instrument (for which preliminary results were presented in September 1999 at the Forum for the Future of Higher Education) reveals that as few as twenty key management behaviors may provide a strong prediction of workplace respect.

This model demonstrates that supervision can do little to influence *directly* workplace cooperation or performance. Rather, the main role of the effective supervisor is to excel in the behaviors that lead to workplace respect—the foundation on which desired organizational patterns and, ultimately, team-based performance critically depends. These behaviors can be improved through goal setting, measurement, and feedback.

Can High-Performance Teams Emerge Without Supervision?

A popular management belief suggests that teams, provided with appropriate resources and empowered by the authority to solve problems as needed to pursue an understood mission, can develop effective patterns with little supervisory influence. This view is heralded as "the organization of the future" by proponents who extol its value in enterprises that must meet rapidly changing market demands through teamwork, collaboration, and information sharing. However, the Irvine model demonstrates the foundational role of supervision in *enabling* teamwork, collaboration, and information sharing, since the key supervisory behaviors are essential to foster workplace respect—the necessary precursor to these patterns of workplace cooperation.

Are These Management Behaviors Innate or Learned?

Are the management behaviors that enable teamwork and team performance learned skills or personality traits? The evidence from UC Irvine is that these behaviors are not inborn, because managers improved significantly when provided with data indicating how supervision was perceived with respect to the key behaviors:

By their employees in the immediate unit

In comparison to other units' supervisors

In relation to organization-wide goals for each measured behavior

Managers were assisted by a consultant to improve in areas where they scored below average or below the goal for a desired behavior. The excellent results— significant improvement overall across all measured behaviors—suggests that codification of performance expectations, measurement, feedback, and goal setting had led to learning and improvement. (Whether a Hawthorne-like effect could explain such consistent, widespread, measured improvement appears doubtful.) The conclusion is that these key management behaviors—including the ones that seem more like traits than acquired skills—are *learned*.

The Value of a Behavioral Model

Managers need to base their actions on a valid model of what employees believe and value and how they can be motivated, especially when innovation and improvement are needed by the enterprise. Intuition and common sense do not consistently provide complete and reliable management insights. For example, without an empirical model, would it be obvious to a manager that expecting and rewarding behaviors in the workplace cooperation construct might prove futile unless he or she evidences behaviors and qualities that (first) foster workplace respect? Without the model, would it be apparent that teamwork is unlikely to develop in the absence of mutual respect in the workplace? These observations may seem intuitive and obvious once revealed by the model, but these causal links are weakly developed in many improvement models.

A validated model provides some assurance that the organization is not rewarding the wrong behaviors, incentivizing the wrong values, or conveying the wrong expectations or conflicting messages. Whether intrinsic or explicit, every improvement protocol embodies a model of how people in a workplace lead, follow, solve problems, and communicate. Moreover, all improvement programs contain inherent values—about what *forms* of leading, following, solving problems, and communicating are expected, tolerated, rewarded, or praised.

The management behavior factors in the model, the workplace respect variables, and the workplace cooperation patterns are worth measuring, adopting as performance goals and expectations, valuing in mission statements, reflecting in unit performance objectives, evaluating in individuals' performance appraisals, incorporating in workshops and training, and rewarding through formal and informal systems of recognition. These behavioral foundations balance and complement (rather than supplant) the "technical" features of a management change model. This balance is important to stimulate *sustainable* change. The most effective technical tools—process redesign techniques, design principles, customer satisfaction and performance measurement systems, benchmarking, and quality standards—become ineffectual unless they are balanced by behavioral elements centered around employee beliefs, values, rewards, incentives, and disincentives (of which many characterize the "informal organization" more than the formal organization).

The worth of a validated model stems from its likely effectiveness in stimulating improved enterprise performance as the values, expectations, and normative behaviors it embodies are fostered. Variables with little predictive value in the model can be essentially ignored, enabling limited resources to be concentrated on the factors that will most likely produce results. In a workplace with limited time and other resources to invest in improvement, especially given the imperative of uninterrupted production, the most efficient management change model is the leanest, simplest one. Moreover, overly complicated management change models are likely to contain inconsistencies and incoherent, mixed messages.

If You Adopt (All or Part of) This Model

The Irvine management change model illustrates how organizational change in the critical areas of workplace respect and cooperation start from a foundation of distinct management behaviors that can be codified as performance expectations. Do not attempt to implement this model without adopting these (or very similar) explicit supervisory and team performance standards, as well as measurement and reward systems to support new performance expectations.

Before implementing this (or any) behavioral model, examine the underlying and inherent values in order to determine whether they are valid in your organization, or your *envisioned* organization. Every behavioral model contains embedded values (whether expressed or not) that will undermine implementation if they clash with mixed messages from other behavioral systems, such as the human resources system (as discussed earlier). Inherent values need to be made explicit and evaluated systematically for both validity and consistency.

It may not be necessary to adopt a management change model as comprehensive as the UC Irvine Model for Sustaining Administrative Improvement. This model's subset of value-based supervisory, cooperation, and respect expectations can be experienced consistently and coherently—as necessary for *sustainable* change—if integrated into performance objectives, performance evaluations, incentive programs, training workshops, measurement systems, recognition and reward systems, and stated goals for the enterprise. At its simplest, the supervisory effectiveness model explained above can be implemented by (1) measuring supervisory behaviors that foster respect in the workplace, (2) determining whether these behaviors lead to cooperation-based outcomes, and (3) if validated, providing data to supervisors and work groups to foster learning and performance improvement.

Sustainable Improvement

Sustainable change requires an empirically validated model that is:

- Balanced, with complementary behavioral and technical tools
- Consistent with (other) belief and value systems of both the formal and informal organization

- Internally coherent, with no conflicting elements that might trigger a retreat to status quo patterns
- Capable of providing clear information about the behaviors that can be improved through measurement and feedback

Models that fall short of these fundamentals or that fail to engage and influence employee belief systems about what is expected, tolerated, rewarded, respected, and considered effective may stimulate positive change but will be short-lived.

Sustainable improvement in enterprise performance patterns requires consistency and coherence in value systems and in all related reward systems because, until new behaviors are embedded in shared values, they are vulnerable to status quo reversion. This is one reason why some enterprise improvement models have more lasting effects than others. The other reason is that many improvement programs—including ones that have the wrappings of sophistication—lack an underlying, empirically validated behavioral model that counterbalances their technical features and *engages* (not merely explains) the dynamic of values, expectations, rewards, disincentives, symbols, motivations, and beliefs that affect individual and team effectiveness.

Index

A

Academic planning, 54–56
Academic work, recognition of, 57
Access to information/technology, 130
Activities, elimination of joint provision of, 108
Activity driven method of cost allocation, 96
Adjunct faculty, 55. *See also* Faculty
Administration, tasks of, 57
Administration and faculty, split between, 53
Adult education, 109, 124n10
Advising, 56–57
Aid to students, policies on, 14
Alliances, 122–123
Allocation methodologies for research funding, 95–96
Alumni, 93, 98–99
Amazon.com, 107, 123, 125n31
American education, 60
Andrew W. Mellon Foundation, 95
Antitrust issues, 11, 46, 121
Apollo Group, 110
Apologia (Arnold), 58

Applicants, choosing similar, 10
Appointment/evaluation of deans, 97–98
Appointment of deans, 97–98
Aptitude: controlling for estimates of earnings, 36–37, 39; increasing returns for those with, 14; and return to attending selective colleges, 28–29
"Architecture for the 21st Century: An Information Technology Strategic Plan for Indiana University," 127. *See also* Information technology (IT) at Indiana University
"Arms race of spending," 89–90
Arnold, Matthew, 58
Arthur D. Little corporate university, 120
Athletes, 74–76, 76–81
Athletic programs by categories of institutions, 70. *See also* Competitive sports
Attitudes of students, 56–57
Attitudes toward sports teams, 83. *See also* Competitive sports
Attracting students, 9, 10

Attractive fields of study, 48
Average SAT scores by college selectivity, 20
Axtell, J., 44

B

Bacon, Francis, 61
Baer, W. S., 123
Bailey, K., 104, 108, 110
Baldridge criteria, 142
Bank of America University, 118–120
Barber, B., 62
Barnes and Noble, 107
Barro, R., 9
Barron's Profiles of American Colleges, 17
Barron's Selectivity Index, 17, 18–19
Basic Educational Opportunity Grant (BEOG), 92
Bate, W. J., 47
Bauer, W., 123
BCG (Boston Consulting Group), 107
Behavioral models, value of, 151–152